ENJOY THE FLAVORS OF CHINESE COOKING

PUBLISHER REPRESENTATIVE OFFICE

UNITED STATES: Prime Communication System

P.O.BOX 456 Shaw Island, WA. 98286

AUTHORS SALES AGENCY: A.K.HARANO COMPANY

P.O.Box 1005 Cypress, CA. 90630

Phone: (714) 739-2755

D&BH ENTERPRISES

94-443 Kahuanani Street Waipahu, HI. 96797

Phone: (808) 671-6041

OVERSEAS DISTRIBUTORS

UNITED STATES: JP TRADING, INC.

300 Industrial Way

Brisbane, Calif. 94005

Phone: (415) 468-0775, 0776

MEXICO:Publicationes Sayrols, S.A. de C.V.
COLOMBIA: Jorge E. Morales & CIA. LTDA.
TAIWAN: Formosan Magazine Press, Ltd.
HONG KONG: Apollo Book Company, Ltd.
THAILAND: Central Department Store Ltd.
SINGAPORE: MPH DISTRIBUTORS (S) PTE, LTD.
MALAYSIA: MPH DISTRIBUTORS SDN, BHD.
PHILIPPINES: National Books Store, Inc.
KOREA: Tongjin Chulpan Muyeok Co, Ltd.
INDONESIA: C.V.TOKO BUKU "MENTENG"
INDIA: Dani Book Land, Bombay 14
AUSTRALIA: BOOKWISE INTERNATIONAL
GUAM, SIPAN AND MICRONESIAN ISLANDS: ISLAND PLANT-LIFE PRODUCTS

ISBN4-915249-45-X

Dedication

To Willkie, Kimberley and Pamela

CONTENTS

INTRODUCTION

同 聲 相 應

The flavors of Chinese cooking are diverse and easy to achieve. The use of a few essential ingredients combined with the use of fresh seasonal ingredients will produce results worthy of any casual or festive occasion.

Preparation of a Chinese meal begins with a thorough understanding of cooking techniques and ingredients. Be sure to read the information section of this book paying special attention to the use of cornstarch for thickening (page 98).

With the exception of a few recipes which are family favorites, the majority of the recipes are Quick and Easy, appropriate for one dish meals which can be served with fresh steamed rice.

Steaming is a very healthy and practical method of cooking which is used very extensively in this book. The recipes are delicious, economical, and very suitable for the lifestyles of today.

I hope these recipes will serve as a guide and with more experince in Chinese cooking you will feel the freedom to create and experiment with other ingredients. You will find the results to be delicious and each meal will be an event to look forward to.

These are the recipes prepared through the years by our parents and enjoyed by countless friends and relatives. The celebrations of life are many and should always include a festive menu. The sharing of food has always been warm and rewarding experience for all of us from simple meals to elegant banquets.

December 1987

Judy Lew

6

ACKNOWLEDGMENTS

To my parents, thank you for your love and guidance through the years. And to my father a special thank you for your thoughtful interpretation of each chapter in your poetic prose.

I would like to thank my publisher Mr. Shiro Shimura for the opportunity to express my love of cooking and teaching in this book.

To Yukiko, thank you very much for the encouragement, dedication and your constant words of wisdom which is appreciated at all times.

My most sincere gratitude to my editors Mr. Naito, Ms.Kasugai, Mr.Sonoda, Ms.Suzuki, Ms.Uchiyama and the marvelous staff at JOIE, Inc. for the invaluable assistance in the final completion of this book.

I am grateful for the opportunity to work with Mr. Tomio Moriguchi, President of Uwajimaya, and for his encouragement.

To my photographer George Nakauye, a very sincere thank you for your patience and expertise so generously shared in the expressions of each photograph.

And to Marc Yamada, your assistance through this project was great. Thank you for your enthusiasm and hard work.

A very special thank you to Hisayo Nakahara for your assistance in the preparation and styling of each recipe. Your creativity and endless supply of energy was so generously shared.

To Elsie Tokita, my appreciation is never ending, thank you always for your readiness to assist me in my projects. Your expertise is always appreciated.

I am indebted to Mike Robinson who got me started. Thank you for setting my computer straight when I needed the help.

METRIC TABLES

★ 1 cup is equivalent to 240 ml in our recipes: (American cup measurement)

    1 American cup=240 ml=8 American fl oz

    1 British cup=200 ml=7 British fl oz

    1 Japanese cup=200 ml

1 tablespoon=15 ml   1 teaspoon=5 ml

T=tablespoon	t=teaspoon	C=Cup
fl=fluid	oz=ounce	lb=pound
ml=milliliter	g=gram	cm=centimeter
F=Fahrenheit	C=Celsius	

TABLES CONVERTING FROM U.S. CUSTOMARY SYSTEM TO METRICS

Liquid Measures

U.S. Customary system	oz	g	ml
1/16 cup=1 T	½ oz	14 g	15 ml
¼ cup=4 T	2 oz	60 g	59 ml
½ cup=8 T	4 oz	115 g	118 ml
1 cup=16 T	8 oz	225 g	236 ml
1 ¾ cups	14 oz	400 g	414 ml
2 cups=1 pint	16 oz	450 g	473 ml
3 cups	24 oz	685 g	710 ml
4 cups	32 oz	900 g	946 ml

Liquid Measures

Japanese system	oz	ml
⅛ cup	⅞ oz	25 ml
¼ cup	1 ¾ oz	50 ml
½ cup	3 ½ oz	100 ml
1 cup	7 oz	200 ml
1 ½ cups	10 ½ oz	300 ml
2 cups	14 oz	400 ml
3 cups	21 oz	600 ml
4 cups	28 oz	800 ml

Weights

ounces to grams
¼ oz = 7 g
½ oz = 14 g
1 oz = 30 g
2 oz = 60 g
4 oz = 115 g
6 oz = 170 g
8 oz = 225 g
16 oz = 450 g

Linear Measures

inches to centimeters
½ in= 1.27 cm
1 in= 2.54 cm
2 in= 5.08 cm
4 in=10.16 cm
5 in=12.2 cm
10 in=25.4 cm
15 in=38.1 cm
20 in=50.8 cm

Temperatures

Fahrenheit (F) to Celsius (C)		
freezer storage	−10°F=	−23 .3°C
	0°F=	17 .7°C
water freezes	32°F=	0 °C
	68°F=	20 °C
	100°F=	37 .7°C
water boils	212°F=	100 °C
	300°F=	148 .8°C
	400°F=	204 .4°C

Deep-Frying Oil Temperatures

300°F−330°F(150°C−165°C)=low
340°F−350°F(170°C−175°C)=moderate
350°F−360°F(175°C−180°C)=high

Conversion Factor

$$C=F-32\times\tfrac{5}{9}$$

$$F=\frac{C\times9}{5}+32$$

BASIC TIPS

These basic tips will save you time and make for the successful preparation of a Chinese Meal.

1. Thoroughly read the first chapter of this book, paying special attention to **Cornstarch for Thickening** portion appearing in the Stir Frying section. Become acquainted with the techniques of cooking and the various equipment available to accomplish this purpose. Always read the entire recipe before you attempt to cook.

2. Organize in advance what you need to do. Decide which dishes can be kept warm and cook those courses first. Have all the required ingredients cut and measured for each dish and arranged on a tray such that everything will be on hand.

3. Slicing meat against the grain of the long muscle fibers will result in added tenderness when the meat is cooked. Partially frozen meat is easier to slice and more uniform slices can be obtained.

4. The use of garlic enhances the flavor of cooked food. With the wide blade of the cleaver, gently hit the clove of garlic, separating the skin which should be removed and discarded. Then crush the garlic with the blade of the cleaver. Crushed garlic may be added to most any dish. Just add the crushed garlic to oil heating in the wok. After the flavor has been released, the garlic may be removed or left in the wok while cooking the rest of the ingredients. Be careful not to burn the garlic.

5. Shaohsing wine and other rice wines may be replaced with dry sherry in most recipes. Recipes calling for mirin, a Japanese sweet rice wine, should not be replaced with Chinese rice wine. Chinese rice wine and mirin are not directly interchangeable.

6. Chicken stock may be used in place of water in recipes other than pastries, doughs, or sweet and sour dishes. This will result in a richer flavor. Canned chicken broth is a good substitute if you do not have time to make your own.

7. Dried forest mushrooms and other dried foods must be soaked in warm water before using in the recipe. They should be soaked until soft, removed, and then rinsed. The usual size of a medium mushroom after soaking is approximately three inches (8cm) in diameter.

8. The recipes contained in this book were tested and developed using **Kikkoman** soy sauce which is considered a medium soy sauce. Use a medium soy sauce unless otherwise specified for best results.

9. A recipe requiring prawns will necessitate the proper shelling and deveining of the prawns. This is done by first removing the transparent shell. Cut open the top of the prawn to expose the black sandy vein. Remove the vein by gently pulling it out. The blue vein underneath the prawn should be left alone. Rinse the prawns and towel dry. Proceed with the recipe.

10. Always use your judgment in the substitution of ingredients called for in a recipe. Most ingredients used in this book are explained in the glossary. Be creative and do not be afraid to adapt the recipes to your own personal tastes.

T=tablespoon   t=teaspoon   C=cup

11. " "a pepper sign denotes a spicy dish.

Dim Sum 食兮壽康

SHRIMP AND PORK DUMPLINGS 蝦餃

SERVE AS A SELECTION IN A BUFFET MEAL OF DIM SUM

"Dim sum,"literally translated, is dot of the heart, but more appropriately should be termed heart's delight.

A dim sum luncheon consists of bite-size meat and vegetable morsels which are steamed, pan fried, deep fried or baked, and served with tea.

INGREDIENTS

Makes 20

Filling

1/3lb(150g)	shrimp, shelled, deveined and chopped
1/3lb(150g)	ground pork
2	black mushrooms, soaked, rinsed and chopped
1/4C	chopped bamboo shoots
1/4C	green peas, or chopped green onions
1T	sesame seed oil
1/2t	sugar
1t	salt
1/2t	white pepper
1	egg white
2T	cornstarch

Dough

1C	wheat starch
1/2C	tapioca starch
1/2t	salt
1C	boiling water
2t	oil

1. Combine filling ingredients and set in refrigerator for 1 hour.
2. In a large pot, combine wheat starch, tapioca starch and salt. Make well in center and pour in rapid boiling water. Stir to moisten ingredients. Cover pot and allow dough to rest 10 minutes.
3. Knead warm dough adding 2 t oil until smooth. Keep covered until ready to use.
4. Roll dough into a rod and cut walnut size pieces. Roll each piece in hand until smooth.
5. Generously oil cleaver and counter top. Press out dough to form a 4 inch (10cm) circle. Put in 1 T filling and close to form a crescent.
6. Place on an oiled steaming plate and steam for 20 minutes.
7. Serve with soy sauce mixed with hot mustard sauce.

① **Combine filling and set in refrigerator.**   ② **Pour boiling water into starch mix and stir.**   ③ **Knead with oil until smooth.**

⑤ **Steam on an oiled steaming plate.**   ④ **Using cleaver, press out dough.**

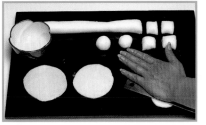

CHICKEN ROLLS 鷄　巻

INGREDIENTS

Makes 25

25	won ton wrappers

Filling

2C	ground chicken
1	Chinese sausage, chopped
2T	chopped onion
1/4C	chopped bean sprouts
1	black mushroom, soaked, rinsed and chopped
1/4C	chopped bamboo shoots
2T	soy sauce
1T	rice wine
1/2t	salt
1T	sesame seed oil
1T	cornstarch
4C	oil for deep frying(350°F / 175°C)

DELICIOUS SERVED WITH ANY VEGETABLE DISH

1. Combine all filling ingredients.
2. Place 2 t filling per wrapper on the lower corner. Fold bottom corner up to cover filling, fold both sides in and roll up wrapper sealing with water.
3. Deep fry for 3 minutes or until golden brown.
4. Serve with sweet and sour sauce or favorite dip (See page 55).

Wrap filling and seal with water

Deep-fry in hot oil for 3 minute

PEARL BALLS 珍珠丸

INGREDIENTS

Makes 18

Meat Mixture

1lb(450g)	lean ground pork
1	Chinese sausage, minced
1/4C	chopped bamboo shoots
1	Chinese mushroom soaked, rinsed chopped
1T	rice wine
1T	soy sauce
1t	salt
2T	cornstarch
1T	sesame seed oil
5	water chestnuts cut into quarters
1C	sweet rice(soaked in water for 1 hour and drained)

SERVE AS A SIDE DISH WITH CHOW MEIN

1. Combine meat mixture.
2. Surround each piece of water chestnut with meat mixture to form a 1½ inch (4cm) ball.
3. Roll each meat ball in sweet rice.
4. Place in steamer and steam for 25 minutes.

＊Food coloring can be added to soaking rice to obtain different colors.

Roll meat mixture into a 1½ inch (4cm) ball centering a each piece of water chestnut. Roll in sweet rice.

Place in steamer and steam for 25 minutes.

FRIED TARO TURNOVERS 芋 角

TRY OTHER FILLING RECIPES FOR VARIATIONS

INGREDIENTS

Makes 10

Filling
1T	oil
1C	ground or diced roast pork
1/4C	diced black mushrooms
1/4C	chopped onions
2T	oyster sauce
1t	sesame seed oil
1t	five spice powder
1T	rice wine
1/2t	salt
1/4C	soup stock
1T	cornstarch

1lb(450g) taro root

2T	cornstarch
1/2C	soup stock

1T	oil
1/2t	salt
1/2c	flour
1	egg, beaten
1C	*panko*

3—4C oil for deep frying(350°F／175℃)

Use cornstarch to dust hands

1. Heat wok, add 1 T oil. Stir fry pork until done. Add remaining ingredients. Cook for ½ minute. Dissolve 1 T cornstarch in soup and add to pork mixture, bring to a boil to thicken sauce. Remove, set aside and refrigerate.
2. Peel rough skin or taro root, rinse root and slice into ½ inch (1.5cm) thick slices. Arrange in a steamer and steam for ½ hour or until tender.
3. Dissolve 2 T cornstarch in ½ C soup stock, bring to a boil; cool.
4. Mash taro and mix in enough of thickened soup stock and oil to resemble thick mashed potatoes. Add salt and mix thoroughly.
5. Take about ¼ C of the taro mixture, form into a round ball and flatten to form a ½ inch (1.5cm) thick round. Dust hands with cornstarch to keep from sticking. Place 1 T filling in turnover and close off top; roll in hands to form an oval shape.
6. Coat outside with flour, dip in egg and roll in *panko*.
7. Deep fry 3—4 minutes or until turnovers are golden brown.

Stir fry pork until done. Cook with remaining filling ingredients.

Peel rough skin of taro root, rinse and slice into 1½ inch (4cm) thick slices.

Steam taro root for ½ hour until tender.

Dissolve 2 T cornstarch in 1½ C Soup stock, bring to a boil. Cool.

Mash taro and mix in enough of thickened soup stock and oil. Add salt and mix thoroughly.

Coat with flour, dip in egg, press in *panko*. Deep fry 3-4 minutes.

Take about 1½ C of the taro mixture, Form into a round ball and flatten. Place 1 T filling in turnover and close off top. Form an oval shape. Dust hands with cornstarch to keep from sticking.

TARO CAKE 芋頭糕

DELICIOUS SERVED WITH "SPICY SPARERIBS" (See page 38)

INGREDIENTS

Meat Filling
1T	oil
¼lb(115g)	boneless pork cut into ½ inch (1.5cm) dice
2	Chinese sausages diced
¼C	diced ham
2T	chopped salted turnip
½t	salt
¼t	five spice powder
1T	rice wine
1T	oil
2C	diced taro root
½t	salt
½C	soup stock

Cake Mixture
1C	cake flour, sifted
¼C	tapioca starch
1½C	chicken stock (See page 73)
¼C	chopped green onions
1T	toasted sesame seeds

1. Heat wok, add 1 T oil. Stir fry pork and sausage until pork turns grey. Add ham, turnip, salt, five spice powder and wine. Stir fry until sauce reduces, remove contents and set aside.
2. Peel taro, slice and dice.
   Heat a clean wok and add 1 T oil. Stir fry *taro* root adding ½ C soup stock. Cover, bring to a boil, reduce temperature to medium high and cook taro for 5 minutes or until soup stock has reduced. Remove and allow to cool.
3. Combine cake flour, tapioca starch and chicken stock in a bowl. Combine mixture thoroughly making sure there are no lumps.
4. Lightly grease a 9 inch (23cm) round cake pan. Place in 1 layer of taro root. Scatter in meat filling. Cover with cake mixture. Repeat process until the pan is full, ending with a scattering of meat mixture.
5. Steam the mixture in a steamer for ½ hour. When cake is done, scatter with green onions or parsley. Sprinkle on sesame seeds.
6. Allow cake to cool before slicing. Traditionally this cake is sliced in diamond shaped pieces. Start by cutting strips 2 inches (5cm) wide. Then make diagonal slices 2 inches (5cm) wide again.

＊Pieces of taro cake are delicious pan fried in a lightly oiled pan.

To fry: Heat thin layer of oil in heavy large skillet over medium heat. Add diamonds(in batches; do not crowd) and fry until heated through and golden brown. Arrange on platter. Sprinkle with onion and sesame seeds. Serve immediately.

Stir fry pork and sausage, Add remaining meat mixture ingredients and cook.

Peel taro, slice and dice.

Stir fry taro root, adding soup stock.

Combine cake mixture ingredients thoroughly.

In greaced cake pan, lay taro and scatter meat filling.

Cover with cake mixure. Repeat proess.

Steam for ½ hour

Sprinkle on green onion and sesame seed.

Dim Sum

Fresh fruits in season also make very nice desserts. A visit to a Chinese bakery if there is one in your area will provide a maximum selection of Chinese dessert items.

EGG CUSTARD TARTS 蛋 韃

CAN BE SERVED AS A DESSERT

INGREDIENTS

18-20 tarts

Custard
1¼C	hot water
½C	sugar
4	eggs
1t	vanilla
1t	vinegar

Pastry
1½C	all purpose flour, sifted
1T	sugar
½C	chilled butter
2T	shortening
1	egg
1t	vanilla

1. Dissolve sugar in hot water, allow to cool and add remaining ingredients.
2. Strain egg mixture. Set aside.
3. Combine flour with sugar. Cut in butter and shortening until mixture resembles coarse meal.
4. Combine egg with vanilla and add to flour mixture. Turn dough onto a lightly floured surface and knead for 30 seconds.
5. Divide dough into 18 pieces and press into 2½ inch (6.5cm) tart pans. Press to ¼ inch (0.7cm) thickness, fluting edge.
6. Arrange tart shells 1 inch (2.5cm) apart on baking sheet. Stir custard mixture, pour into each shell. Bake at 375°F (190°C) for 20 minutes. Serve hot or cool.

To make custard ① Mix custard ingredients and stir well.

② Strain mixture and set aside.

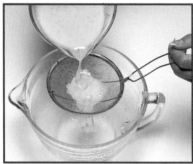

③ Knead into a smooth. On a floured board, knead for 30 seconds.

To make pastry ① Cut butter in flour, sugar and shortening.

② Add egg with vanilla into mixture.

④ Place dough into tart pans, fit into tart pan and flute edge.

Dim Sum

Most restaurants usually serve dim sum between the hours of 11:00 A.M. to 3:00 P.M. Carts filled with the appetizers are constantly circulated throughout the restaurant. Stop the waitress and make your selections. After the meal, the small plates are counted and totalled. Eat slowly and enjoy!

FORTUNE COOKIES 簽語餅

FUN ENDING TO ANY MEAL

INGREDIENTS

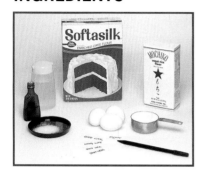

Makes 25

1C	cake flour, sifted
3T	sweet rice flour(or cornstarch)
½C	sugar
¼t	salt
½C	vegetable oil
3	egg whites
¼C	water
1t	vanilla extract

Paper fortunes

1. Combine cake flour, sweet rice flour, sugar and salt in a bowl, set aside.
2. In a large bowl, combine oil, egg whites, water and vanilla. Beat on medium speed for 1 minute.
3. Mix in dry ingredients and blend until smooth.
4. Drop 1 T batter onto a lightly oiled cookie sheet. Spread batter with a spoon in a circular motion to a 4 inch (10cm) round.
5. Bake 15—20 minutes at 325°F (163℃) or until light brown.

6. Remove cookies one at a time from oven. Place fortune on cookie, fold in half and quickly bend on the edge of a can. Place in a muffin pan to keep cookies in shape.

∗Bake only a few cookies at a time.

∗If cookies harden before folding, reheat in oven. Wear cloth gloves if cookies are too hot to handle. For even browning, use a dark, heavy cookie sheet.

Combine cake flour, sweet rice flour, sugar and salt.

Combine oil, egg white, water and vanilla. Blend with dry ingredients.

Spread batter with spoon.

Place fortune on cookie, fold in half and quickly bend.

Place in a muffin pan to keep cookie from unfolding.

Fortunes on paper

♥GOOD HEALTH AND HAPPINESS WILL ALWAYS COME YOUR WAY.
♥GOOD TIMES ARE ALWAYS SHAR- ED.
♥GOOD FORTONE WILL BE YOURS FOREVER.
♥ENJOY EACH MOMENT OF LIFE TO THE FULLEST

*Meat*Poultry 色味香美

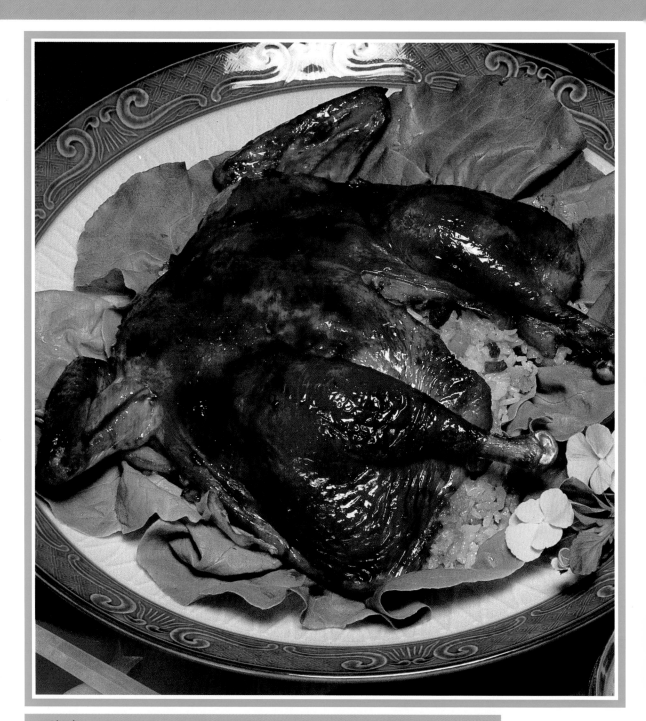

STUFFED BONELESS CHICKEN

釀　鷄

SERVE WITH STIR FRIED VEGETABLE DISH

Poultry dishes may be combined with vegetables, but will also often be found standing alone as a main course.

INGREDIENTS

1   3 lb(1.350g)fryer chicken boned,

Marinade
¼C	soy sauce
2T	rice wine
2T	sugar
1t	grated ginger
2	cloves garlic, minced

1   recipe of **JEWELED RICE,** page 94 **or STEAMED GLUTI-NOUS RICE** page 96

1T	soy sauce
1T	*mirin*

1. Place chicken on cutting board, breast side down and cut through skin along the back bone. Start cutting and scrapping meat away from bones. When you come to the wing joint, cut through joint and continue to breast bone.
2. Continue to release meat from the back until the thigh bone is reached. Twist back and cut through joint. Now cut and release meat to the breast bone.
3. Bone other side of chicken in the same manner. Snap breast bone and pull of meat. Be careful not to puncture skin.
4. Rinse chicken and dry with paper towels. Place chicken in marinade and allow to marinate in refrigerator for at least 1 hour or overnight
5. Prepare 1 recipe of JEWELED RISE using glutinous rice instead of calrose rice. (Calrose rice can be used if a less sticky filling is desired).
6. Cover the top of a broiling pan with foil and puncture holes in foil to match rack. Coat surface of foil with non-stick spray. Place rack back on top of pan and ¼ inch (0.7cm) of water to bottom pan.
7. Mound rice mixture on rack and cover with chicken, shaping to resemble a whole chicken. (Chicken can be stuffed and the back sewn closed). Roast chicken immediately stuff and roast at 350°F (175℃) for 1½ hours or until thickest part of chicken registers 175°F (80℃). Baste with soy sauce and *mirin*.
8. Allow chicken to sit for 10 minutes. Carefully loosen meat and rice from foil and slide onto serving platter.

＊Stuff chicken just before roasting.

Breast side down and cut through skin along the back bone.

Cut and scrap meat away from bones.

Snap breast bone and pull meat.

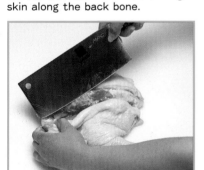

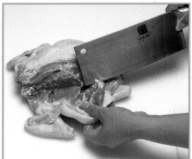

Marinade chicken in refrigerator for at least 1 hour or overnight.

Mound **JEWELED RICE** on rack.

Cover with chicken and roast imm-dietry.

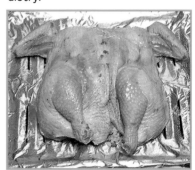

STUFFED CHICKEN BREASTS

THIS CAN BE SERVED AS AN APPETIZER　　釀鷄胸

INGREDIENTS

Serves 4

2	large whole chicken breasts
1t	grated ginger
2t	rice wine
½t	salt, pepper

Filling

½C	prawns, shelled, deveined and chopped
½C	ground pork
¼C	chopped mushrooms
2T	chopped bamboo shoots
¼C	chopped green onions
1t	grated ginger root
½t	salt
1T	cornstarch
½	egg white

Breading

½C	all purpose flour
1	egg beaten
1C	*panko*(dehydrated bread crumbs)

3C　oil for deep frying(375°F／190°C)

Shredded lettuce for garnish

Serve with five spice salt or Szechuan pepper salt

1. Remove bones from chicken breast (refer to information section—page100)
2. Lay chicken breast flat and cut into halves. Butterfly each half by slicing breast from the outer edge, part way through, to open like a book. (Halves will resemble a whole breast, but thinner).
3. Rub each half with ginger, wine, salt and pepper. Combine all filling ingredients and press onto top of chicken pieces.
4. Carefully coat each piece with flour, egg and press on *panko.*
5. Deep fry at 375°F (190°C) for 5 minutes, turning to brown evenly. Cut chicken into bite—size pieces and serve on top of shredded lettuce.

＊Wet fingers with water to smooth top of filling.

＊Cut cooked chicken into small pieces and serve as appetizers.

＊Mix sliced almonds with *panko* and coat chicken before frying for almond breaded chicken.

Lay chicken breast flat and cut into halves.

Buttter fly each half by slicing breast from the outer edge, part way through, to open like a book.

Press filling onto top of chicken pieces.

Gently coat each piece with flour,
egg and press on *panko*.

Deep fry at **375°F** (**190°C**),
turning to brown evenly.

CHICKEN WITH MUSHROOMS

SERVE WITH HOT RICE

毛菇鷄

INGREDIENTS

Serves 4-6
½lb(225g) boneless chicken sliced

Marinade
1T	soy sauce
1T	sesame seed oil
1T	rice wine
1T	cornstarch
2T	oil
½C	sliced onions
1C	pea pods
½C	sliced carrots
1C	sliced fresh mushrooms
3	black mushrooms, soaked and sliced (simmer for 10 minutes in soup stock)
1C	canned straw mushrooms, drained
½C	chicken stock
½t	salt
	Cornstarch and water to thicken

1. Combine chicken with marinade.
2. Heat a wok, add oil. Stir fry chicken until done, remove and set aside. Add all vegetables and mushrooms. Stir to combine, add chicken stock and salt.
3. Bring to a boil, return chicken to wok and thicken with cornstarch and water.

＊Other vegetables may be added.

All ingredients are prepared.

CHICKEN WITH PEANUTS 花生鷄丁

INGREDIENTS

Serves 4-6

1lb(450g) chicken breast or thighs
Marinade
2t	rice wine
2t	sesame seed oil
1T	cornstarch

2C	oil(350°F / 175℃)
½C	blanched peanuts(skins removed)

6—8	dried red chili peppers

2cloves	garlic, minced
2t	minced ginger
¼C	each diced green pepper, red pepper
1T	each hot bean paste, rice wine
1T	soy sauce
2t	rice vinegar
½t	sugar
1T	sesame seed oil

SERVE WITH "LEMON FISH" (See page 51)

1. Remove bones from chicken and dice(See page100). Combine with marinade.
2. Heat 2 C oil in wok to 350°F(175℃) and slowly fry peanuts until light brown. Remove and set aside.
3. Carefully pour out oil leaving 2 T. Fry chili peppers in oil until the peppers turn dark brown. Add chicken and stir fry on high heat until all of the meat has turned white.
4. Add garlic, ginger, red and green peppers; stir fry for 1 minute on high. Add remaining ingredients and thoroughly combine reducing sauce.
5. Toss in peanuts, quickly combine and remove to serving plate.

Fry peanuts until light brown. / Fry chili peppers in 2 T oil.

After peppers turn dark brown, add chicken. / Finally toss in peanuts and combine.

BLACK BEAN SAUCE CHICKEN

豆豉鷄

SERVE WITH "STEAMED SALMON WITH GINGER" (See page 50)

INGREDIENTS

Rinse and coarsely chop blank beans.
Slice onion and peppers. Mince ginger.

Serves 4

1lb(450g)	chicken cut into 1 inch(2.5cm) pieces

Marinade

1t	minced ginger
1clove	garlic, minced
½t	sugar
1T each	soy sauce, cornstarch
1C	oil
¼C	black beans, rinsed and coarsely chopped
1clove	garlic, minced
2slices	ginger, minced
½t each	sugar, crushed red chili pepper
1	small onion, sliced
½	green pepper, sliced
½	red pepper, sliced
2T each	rice wine, soy sauce

1. Combine chicken with marinade. Heat wok, add 1 C oil. Stir fry chicken on high heat until golden brown, approximately 5 minutes. Reduce temperature if necessary. Remove chicken, drain and set aside.
2. Heat a clean wok until hot. Add 2 T oil stir fry black beans for ½ minute. Add garlic, ginger, sugar and chili pepper; cook for ½ minute more.
3. Add remaining vegetables, rice wine and soy sauce. Return chicken to wok and reduce liquid.

Combine chicken with marinade.

Stir fry chicken on high heat until golden brown.

Remove chicken, drain and set aside.

Finally, return chicken to wok.

Stir fry

This technique can be applied to any combination of meats and vegetables. Seafood is also delicious.

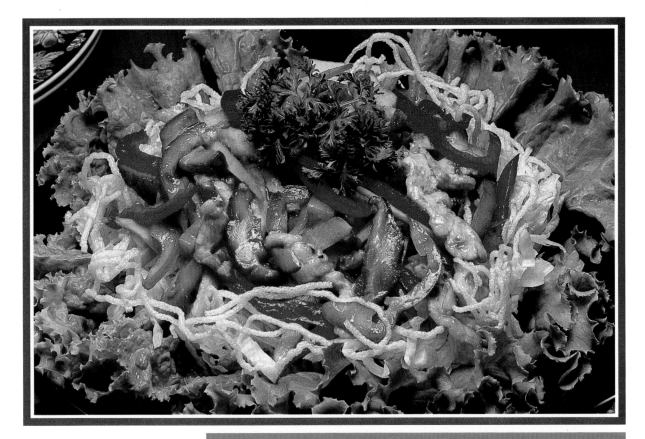

INGREDIENTS

Just prpared ingredients

1lb(450g) boneless chicken breast sliceed thin against the grain

Marinade
1T	each soy sauce, rice wine
1clove	garlic crushed
1t	grated ginger root
½t	sugar
1t	crushed red chili pepper
1T	cornstarch

4C	oil (375°F / 190°C)

2oz(60g)	maifun noodles

2T	oil
3	black mushrooms, soaked, rinsed and sliced thin
½C	thin sliced bamboo shoots
½C	thin sliced green or red pepper
½C	slivered carrots
½t	salt
2t	hot soy bean paste
3T	hoisin sauce
2T	soy sauce
1T	each rice wine, sesame seed oil

6C	shredded green lettuce

SPICY CHICKEN WITH MAIFUN

米粉五香鷄

SERVE AS A COMPLETE MEAL

1. Combine chicken with marinade and allow to marinate ½ hour or longer.
2. Heat 4 C oil in wok and deep fry maifun, small handful at a time. Remove and set aside. Press on maifun to break into shorter lengths.
3. Heat a clean wok and add 2 T oil, stir fry chicken on high heat until done; approximately 3—4 minutes.
4. Add all vegetables and seasonings. Thoroughly combine.
5. Arrange shredded lettuce on large platter. Spread maifun over lettuce. Mound cooked chicken over maifun.

∗ This dish is delicious hot or cold.
∗ Slivered cooked barbecued pork can be used instead of chicken.

Deep fry maifun, remove and break into shorter lengths.

Stir fry chicken for 3—4 minutes. Add all vegetables and seasonings.

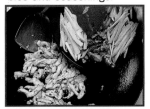

INGREDIENTS

Prepare ingredients.

Serves 4

1lb(450g) boneless chicken(breast or thighs)
2T   cornstarch

Sauce
1/4C   soy sauce
1teach   sesame seed oil, rice wine
1T   sugar
1/2t   grated fresh ginger root
1clove   garlic, finely minced

Sliced Vegetables
1C   zucchini sliced 1/4 inch(0.7cm) thick
1C   carrots sliced 1/4 inch(0.7cm) thick
1C   sliced fresh mushrooms
1C   broccoli, cauliflower, green pepper, or any combination
        of vegetables
4   squares of heavy duty aluminum foil 12 inch(30cm) $\times$ 12
        inch(30cm) or parchment paper

FOIL WRAPPED CHICKEN

錫紙包鷄

SERVE WITH ANY RICE DISH

1. Slice chicken against the grain into ½ inch (1.5cm) thick slices. Mix corn-starch with chicken.
2. Mix together sauce and add to chicken. Allow to marinate ½ hour.
3. Place selection of vegetables in center of each sheet of foil. Place chicken pieces on top of vegetables and spoon remaining sauce over chicken, dividing ingredients equally.
4. Bring 4 corners of foil up to meet at top, seal sides of package by folding edges.
5. Place packages on a cookie sheet and bake in a preheated oven (375°F／190℃) for 25 minutes.
6. Serve with steamed white rice.

＊Other meats or vegetables may be substituted.

＊Entire dish can be steamed, arrange chicken in center of heat proof plate surrounded by vegetables. Steam for ½ hour.

Slice chicken against the grain into 1½ inch (1.5cm) thick slices.

To make packages

Place vegetables, chicken, and sauce in center of each sheet of foil.

Bring 4 corners of foil up to meet at top.

Seal sides of package by folding edges.

STEAMED BLACK BEAN SAUCE SPARERIBS

DELICIOUS WITH HOT RICE

豆豉蒸排骨

The meat is usually shredded, sliced, or cubed into succulent bite-sized pieces for convenient serving.

INGREDIENTS

Chop black beans. Cut ribs into separate pieces between bones

Serves 4

1½lbs(675g)	pork spareribs, cut into 1½inch(4cm) pieces
2T	black beans, rinsed and chopped
2cloves	garlic, minced
1t	minced ginger root
2t	soy sauce
¼t	salt
1t	sugar
2t	crushed red chili pepper
2T	cornstarch

Chopped green onions for garnish

1. Rinse spareribs and thoroughly dry with paper towels. Cut ribs into separate pieces between bones.
2. Place spareribs in a heat proof dish with a rim. Combine with remaining ingredients and place in a steamer. Steam for 30 minutes. Garnish with green onions.

＊Boneless pork cubes, chicken can be used.

Place ingredients in a heat proof dish with a rim.

Steam for 30 minutes.

Meats

Meats should always be sliced against the grain to be the most tender. Marinate with wine, soy sauce, garlic, ginger, oil, cornstarch and other ingredients to achieve different flavors.

BARBECUE PORK WITH PLUM SAUCE

INGREDIENTS

＊This pork roast is delicious cooked in an outdoor barbecue.
Place pork on rack over drip pan. Charcoals should be placed on the sides of barbecue, cover and roast according to barbecue instructions.

TRY ROASTING OUTDOORS IN A CHARCOAL BARBECUE

义燒蘇梅醬

Serves 4-8

12lb(900g)boneless pork loin roast

Marinade
2t	salt
2T	sugar
1t	minced garlic
2t	minced ginger
3T	soy sauce
1/4C	minced onion
1/2t	white pepper
1/2t	five spice
1T	finely minced tangerine peel (soak peel before mincing)

Basting Sauce
1/2C	plum sauce
1T	rice wine
1T	soy sauce

1. Rub pork roast with marinade. Marinate at least 2 hours or over night in refrigerator.

2. Place roast on a rack over some water in a roasting pan. Bake at 350°F(175℃) for approximately 1 hour and 15 minutes.

3. Baste with sauce frequently. Roast is done when temperature registers 175 °F (80℃).

Marinate.

Marinate.

Bake at 350°F (175°C).

Baste with sauce frequently.

STEAMED PORK WITH SZECHUAN VEGETABLE 川菜蒸豬肉

THIS IS A VERY EASY AND DELICIOUS MEAL TO SERVE WITH WHITE RICE

INGREDIENTS

Serves 4

1lb(450g)	boneless pork, sliced thin against the grain
½C	sliced Szechuan preserved vegetable (rinse off chili pepper before slicing)
½t	sugar
1T	soy sauce
1T	cornstarch
	Szechuan pepper powder (see page 36)
	Chinese parsley

1. Place pork in heat proof dish with a rim. Combine pork with sliced preserved vegetable. Mix in sugar, soy sauce and cornstarch.
2. Place in steamer, cover and steam for 20 minutes.
3. Remove contents to serving plate and garnish with a few shakes of pepper and Chinese parsley.

＊Ground pork can be used instead of sliced pork. All ingredients can be chopped together and steamed as a large meat patty.
＊Chicken can be used instead of pork.
＊Add vegetables such as mushrooms, carrots, peas, broccoli towards the end of steaming time to create a one dish meal.

Place ingredients in a heat proof dish with a rim.

Steam for 20 minutes.

SPICED SPARERIBS 五香排骨 🌶

CAN BE SERVED AS AN APPETIZER

Serves 4

1½lbs(675g) pork rib chops

Marinade
1T	hot bean paste
1T	soy sauce
1T	sesame seed oil
½t	five spice powder
1T	rice wine
½t	salt
1t	sugar
3T	cornstarch
1T	Szechuan pepper
4C	oil for deep frying (350°F/175°C)

Cut rib chops with a heavy cleaver. Combine with marinade.

1. With a heavy cleaver, cut rib chops into 2 inch (5cm) pieces.
2. Combine spareribs with marinade; cover and set aside for ½ hour or longer.
3. Lightly toast peppercorns in a skillet.
4. Grind peppercorns to a fine powder. Strain powder of hard pieces of shell.
5. Heat oil and deep fry spareribs for approximately 5 minutes. Serve with Szechuan pepper.

How to make Szechuan pepper corn Grind toasted peppercorn to a fine powder. Strain powder of hard pieces of shell.

Deep fry spareribs for approximately 5 minutes.

SWEET AND SOUR SPICED SPARERIBS

SERVE WITH CHINESE BROCCOLI WITH
OYSTER SAUCE

甜酸五香排骨

INGREDIENTS

Serves 4

1   recipe of **SPICED SPARERIBS** (page 36)

Sweet and Sour Sauce
⅓C   rice vinegar
⅓C   water
1T   cornstarch
2T   soy sauce
¼C   sugar

1T   oil
6   red chili peppers
1C   Chinese pickled vegetables and ginger

Other optional garnishes; tomato,
pineapple, kiwi fruit, red or green
pepper

Bring contents to a full boil,   mix in
cooked spareribs.

1.   Prepare one recipe of SPICED SPARERIBS.
2.   Combine sauce ingredients and set aside
3.   Heat wok,   add oil and fry chilies until brown.   Add pickled vegetables
     and ginger.   Add sauce and bring contents to a full boil. Mix in
     cooked spareribs and quickly toss together.

∗ Serve in pineapple bowl with assorted garnishes.
∗ Boneless pork cubes can be substituted for spareribs.

TWICE COOKED PORK 回爐肉

SERVE WITH "STEAMED STUFFED *TOFU*" (See page 69)

INGREDIENTS

Serves 4-6

½lb(225g)boneless pork roast

2 slices	ginger
1	green onion
1T	oil
1C	cubed green and red pepper or leeks diagonally sliced

Sauce

1t	minced ginger
2cloves	garlic, minced
1T	hot soy bean paste
1T	soy sauce
1T	hoisin sauce
1t	sugar
2T	rice wine

1. In a large pot, bring enough water to a boil to cover pork roast. Place pork roast, ginger and green onion in pot and simmer for ½ hour. Remove and allow to cool.
2. Slice pork into 2 inch (5cm) × 1½ inch (4cm) × ¼ inch (0.7cm) thick slices.
3. Heat wok and add 1 T oil. Stir fry peppers for ½ minute; remove and set aside.
4. Add pork slices and fry pork on high heat until light brown. Drain excess oil from wok if pork was very high in fat.
5. Add all sauce ingredients and stir fry for 1 minute or until sauce is reduced.
6. Return peppers to wok and combine.

＊Serve with a light sprinkling of Szechuan pepper powder(see page 36).

① Simmer pork roast with ginger and green onion for ½ hour.

② Remove and allow to cool.

③ Slice pork and vegetables.

④ Stir fry peppers, remove and set aside.

⑤ Fry pork on high heat.

⑥ Add all sauce ingredients and fry 1 minute or until sauce is reduced.

⑦ Return peppers to wok and combine.

Meats

Stir fry the meat first in the wok with a small amount of oil. Remove meat, then cook vegetables adding the meat back in to retain tenderness without over cooking the meat. This technique is often used when the meat and vegetables require different cooking times.

SPICY STEAK 五香市的

SERVE WITH A STIR FRIED VEGETABLE

INGREDIENTS

Prepare steak and vegetables.

Slice beef into ½ inch (1.5cm) thick by 2 inch (5cm) long slices

Serves 4-6

½lb(225g) flank steak

Marinade
1T	soy sauce
1T	rice wine
1t	grated ginger
1clove	garlic, minced
½t	sugar
2T	cornstarch
2T	oil
¼C	chives cut in 1inch(2.5cm) lengtns
6	dried red chili peppers
1t	minced ginger
1clove	garlic, minced
3T	catsup
1T	brown sugar
1t	rice vinegar
1T	hot bean paste
1T	rice wine
1	tomato cut into wedges

1. Slice beef into ½ inch (5cm) thick by 2 inch (5cm) long slices. Combine with marinade and set aside for ½ hour.
2. Heat wok, and 1 T oil add quickly stir fry chives for ½ minute; remove and set aside. Add 1 T oil to wok and fry chili peppers until brown. Add beef and stir fry very quickly on very high heat until done.
3. Push beef to side of wok and add remaining ingredients to center of wok and bring to a boil. Reduce sauce and stir in beef. Add tomato wedges and chives.

Combine beef with marinade and set aside for ½ hour.

Stir fry chives for ½ minute; remove and set aside.

Finally add tomato wedges and chives.

STEAMED BEEF WITH BROCCOLI

FOR AN EASY ONE DISH MEAL

芥蘭滑牛肉

INGREDIENTS

Serves 4-6

½lb(225g)beef, sliced thin
against the grain

Marinade
2T   soy sauce
1T   rice wine
½t   sugar
1clove garlic, minced
1t   minced ginger root
1T   cornstarch
1T   sesame seed oil
1T   oyster sauce (optional)

2—3C   broccoli floweretes

1   Combine sliced beef with marinade in a heat proof dish with a rim.
2. Place in steamer and steam for 10 minutes.
3. Remove cover and arrange broccoli around outer edge of plate. Cover and steam 10 minutes more.
4. Serve with hot white rice.

∗This is one of my favorite meals to serve on busy evenings.
The entire dish can be prepared ahead. Just steam the meal and start the rice in rice cooker at the same time.
∗Other meats and vegetables can be used for variety.

Combine sliced beef with marinade in a heat proof dish with a rim.

Place in steamer and steam for 10 minutes.

Arrange broccoli, steam 10 minutes more.

Seafood 唇齒留香

FISH HOT POT 魚球煲

SERVE WITH HOT RICE

Nowhere is the importance of bringing out the natural flavor of food more evident than in the preparation of fish and shellfish. The key to delicious seafood is freshness.

INGREDIENTS

Vegetables are assembled

Cut celery cabbage into 3 inch (8cm) pieces. Slice Chestnuts greens onions, black mushrooms, water chestnuts and bamboo shoots. Slice carrots, shape into fish.

Serves 4

1/2 lb(225g)	boneless fish
1/2 t	salt
1T	rice wine
1/8 t	white pepper
1/2	egg white
2T	cornstarch
3—4C	oil for deep frying (350°F/190°C)
1T	oil
6	dried red chili peppers
1/4C	sliced onions
1/4C	sliced black mushrooms (dried must be soaked and rinsed)
1/4C	sliced water chestnuts
1/4C	bamboo shoots
1/8C	sliced carrots (fish shape)
2T	oyster sauce
1T	soy sauce
3/4C	soup stock
1T	cornstarch
3 leaves	celery cabbage cut into 3 inch (8cm) pieces
1C	sliced Chinese greens
1T	sesame seed oil
1	green onion, sliced

Coat fish.

1. Thoroughly dry fish with paper towels and cut into 2 inch (5cm) pieces. Coat fish with salt, wine and pepper. Combine with egg white and cornstarch.

2. Deep fry fish in hot oil for 2 minutes or until golden brown. Remove and set aside.

Deep fry fish and remove.

3. Heat a clean wok, add 1 T oil and fry chilies until brown. Add onions, mushrooms, water chestnuts, bamboo shoots, carrots, oyster sauce and soy sauce.

4. Combine soup stock with cornstarch and add to wok. Bring mixture to a full boil. Add remaining ingredients, return fried fish to wok.

5. Remove contents to a hot pot. Cover and simmer for 1—2 minutes and serve immediately.

Simmer.

GINGER ONION CRAB 羌葱蟹

SERVE WITH "CHICKEN WITH GREENS" (See page 59)

INGREDIENTS

Prepare vegetables.

Slice onion, sliver ginger and slice green onions diagonally.

1	fresh crab (approximately 3 lbs／1,350g)
3T	oil
¼C	slivered ginger
2cloves	garlic, minced
1	medium onion sliced
1T	coarse chopped fermented black beans (or use hot black bean sauce)
¼C	rice wine
2T	soy sauce
2	green onions sliced

1. Break top shell of crab ; clean crab and drain. Cut body in half and separate each leg with a section of the body. Make a small crack on each leg with handle of cleaver. Rinse crab and drain.
2. Heat wok, add 3 T oil and stir fry ginger, garlic and onions until fragrant. Add crab and black beans. Continue to fry for approximately 3 minutes, stirring constantly.
3. Add wine and soy sauce, cover wok and reduce temperature. Cook crab for 3 minutes more, adding more wine if necessary. Toss in green onions just before serving.

∗ The shell of crab can be cooked and retained for garnish.
∗ Serve with lemon soy sauce dip (mix ¼ C soy sauce and ¼ C lemon juice) or ground Szechuan pepper (see page 36).

To prepare crab

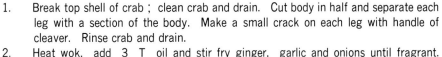

Remove outer shell of crab and discard. Rinse and clean crab. Cut crab in half. Holding each leg by the cavity, break off a section of the center cavity with each leg. Crack legs, rinse off bits of shell, drain and set aside.

① Stir fry ginger, garlic and onions until fragrant.

② Add crab.

③ Add black beans and continue to fry.

④ Add seasonings, cover wok and cook. Toss in green onions just before serving.

FISH WITH BLACK BEAN SAUCE

DELICIOUS WITH ANY STIR FRIED VEGETABLE

豆豉魚

INGREDIENTS

Vegetables are assembled.

Serves 4

1½lbs(685g)	fish fillet or steak
2T	cornstarch
1—2T	oil

Sauce

2T	black beans, rinsed and chopped
2cloves	garlic, minced
1t	minced ginger root
2T	soy sauce
¼t	salt
1t	sugar
2t	crushed red chili pepper
⅓C	rice wine
2T	silvered ginger
	Chopped green onions for garnish
1T	sesame seed oil (optional, pour over fish)

1. Rinse fish and dry thoroughly with paper towels.
2. Coat fish with cornstarch. Place oil in frying pan. Pan fry fish until light brown on one side, then turn and lightly brown other side.
3. Add black beans, garlic and ginger. Add remaining sauce ingredients and wine. Cover and cook gently for 3—4 minutes or until fish is cooked and some of the sauce has reduced.
4. Garnish with ginger, green onions, extra soy sauce and sesame seed oil.

＊Fish can be steamed with sauce ingredients spread over fish. Place in heat proof dish and steam for 10 minutes per inch of thickness of fish.

① After pan frying both sides, add black beans, garlic, and ginger.

② Add remaining sauce ingredients and wine. Cover and cook gently.

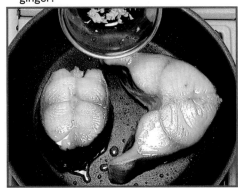

Tea

Tea is the traditional drink served immediately before and after a Chinese meal. The choice of tea is entirely up to individiual tastes. There are basically three groups of teas.

Green tea — unfermented, dried in the sun. Delicate flavor and is light in color.

Oolong tea — Partially fermented green tea imparting a slightly stronger flavor.

Red or Black tea — fermented teas which are first dried in the sun and then fired over charcoal. They possess the strongest flavor among the three varieties of tea.

The scented teas of which jasmine tea is by far the most popular, are made mostly from partially fermented tea.

Tea is properly brewed in porcelain pots and cups. Clean and heat the teapot by pouring in brisk boiling water and waiting until the teapot is warm before discarding the water. Next, add tea leaves and pour in fresh boiling water. Allow the covered tea to steep for approximately three minutes. The tea leaves may be reused for a second or even third brewing, but remember to leave some tea in the pot for the next brewing in order for the tea to release its full aroma.

Any tea will taste harsh and bitter if brewed too strong. The proportion of tea leaves to water will vary with the types of tea and the strength desired. Test a tea by varying the proportion of tea leaves to water until the desired taste is achieved. Do not brew the tea too strong, as Chinese tea drinkers do not add cream or sugar to their tea.

STEAMED FISH
WITH PORK 豬肉蒸魚

SERVE WITH "SPICY EGGPLANT"(See page 63)

INGREDIENTS

Serves 4

1½lbs(685g)	fresh fish fillet or steaks
¼t	salt
½lb(225g)	boneless pork
3—4	black mushrooms, soaked and rinsed
25	tiger lily buds, soaked, rinsed
1T	rice wine
2T	soy sauce
2t	cornstarch
2T	slivered ginger
2T	soy sauce
1T	sesame seed oil (optional)
	Slivered green onions for garnish

How to prepare tiger lily buds.

Soak in warm water about 15 minutes and rinse. Remove any hard knobs. Tie knots.

Prepare ingredients.

Slice pork and mushrooms in thin slivers. Tie knots in tiger lily buds. Sliver ginger.

Combine pork, mushrooms and tiger lily buds with rice wine, soy sause, cornstarch and ginger.

Spread pork mixture over fish and steam.

1. Rinse fish and dry with paper towels. Place fish in heat proof plate with a rim. Sprinkle with salt.
2. Slice pork and mushrooms. Remove any hard knobs on tiger lily buds, tie knots if desired.
3. Combine pork, mushrooms and tiger lily buds with rice wine, soy sauce, cornstarch and ginger.
4. Spread pork mixture over fish in an even layer. Place in steamer and steam for ½ hour.
5. Pour soy sauce over fish, sesame seed oil if desired and garnish with green onions.

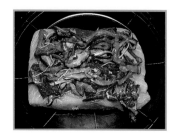

*Fish can be steamed this way without meat mixture. Steam fish until done. Pour off liquid and season with ¼ cup soy sauce poured over fish. Sprinkle ginger and green onion slivers over fish and pour on hot oil.

Wine

Wine served with a Chinese meal is a mere accompaniment to the diversity of flavors in Chinese foods. Shaohsing wine, a rice wine, served warm in porcelain cups, is the most popular wine. However, with so many good Western and European wines to select from, serve what appeals to the palates of you and your guests.

STEAMED SALMON WITH GINGER

CAN USE OTHER FISH FOR VARIATIONS

羌蒸沙面魚

INGREDIENTS

Serves 4

1lb(450g) salmon steak or fillet
2T   slivered fresh ginger
1/8t   white pepper
1/4C   soy sauce
1T   sesame seed oil
1   green onion sliced in diagonal slivers

2T   oil (heated until hot)

Garnish
Chinese parsley, shredded cucumbers, red peppers

Scatter ginger on top of salmon ; steam.

Sizzle ingredients with hot oil.

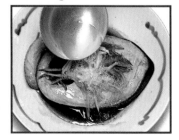

1. Place salmon in a heat proof plate with a rim. Scatter ginger on top of salmon. Place in steamer and steam for 10 minutes per inch (2.5cm) of thickness of fish.
2. Remove fish from steamer, drain liquid from plate.
3. Spread remaining ingredients on top of fish.
4. Sizzle ingredients with hot oil. Serve immediately.
∗ This recipe can be used with any fish. whole fish can be steamed adjusting cooking time and sauce ingredients on top of salmon.

LEMON FISH 檸檬魚

SERVE WITH A SIDE OF VEGETABLES

INGREDIENTS

Serves 4

1lb(450g)	fish fillet
½T	salt
2t	rice wine
½C	flour
1	egg, beaten
1C	*panko* (dehydrated bread crumbs)
3C	oil for deep frying (375°F/190°C)

Lemon Sauce

½C	water
1½T	cornstarch
⅓C	lemon juice
⅓C	sugar
1t	soy sauce
1t	catsup
1t	crushed dried chili pepper (optional)

Garninh
lemon zest, lemon slices and lettuce

1. Sprinkle fish with salt and wine. Rub into fish. Coat fish with flour, dip into egg and press on *panko*.
2. Deep fry until golden brown approximately 4 minutes.
3. Arrange on serving plate.
4. Bring lemon sauce to a full boil, stirring constantly. Pour sauce over fish or serve along side. Garnish with lettuce and lemon.

Coat with flour, dip into egg and press on *Panko*.

Deep fry until golden brown.

Bring lemon sauce to a full boil, stirring constantly.

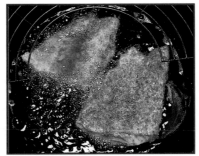

FISH PATTIES 魚 餅

STEAM PATTIES FOR VARIATION

INGREDIENTS

Prepare ahead.

Chop green onion, mushrooms and soaked tangerine peel. Grate ginger. Slice fish.

Serves 4

1lb(450g)	boneless fish fillet
1/4lb(115g)	shrimp (shelled and deveined)
1/4C	sliced black mushrooms, minced
1t	grated fresh ginger root
1/4C	chopped green onions
1t	chopped tangerine peel (soak peel until soft in hot water before chopping)
1T	rice wine
1T	sesame seed oil
1/4t	white pepper
1/2t	salt
2T	cornstarch
1	egg white
2T	oil

1. Combine fish, shrimp, ginger root, green onions and tangerine peel; mince together until a smooth paste is formed using the cleaver.
2. Add remaining ingredients except 2 T oil and thoroughly combine.
3. Divide contents into 4 equal and shape into ½ inch (1.5cm) thick patties.
4. Heat a skillet until hot and lightly coat with oil.
5. Slowly pan fry patties on medium high heat for 3 minutes, turn patties and fry 3 more minutes.
6. Slice patties and serve with soy sauce or your favorite dip.

＊Patties may also be steamed. Shape into balls and cook in soup or deep fry.

Mince fish mixture until a smooth paste in formed.

Add remaining ingredients except 2 T oil and combine.

Divide contents and shape into patties.

Slowly pan fry patties on medium high heat.

CHICKEN AND CRAB STUFFED SHRIMP

INGREDIENTS

Carrot flowers

Slice carrot into 1⁄8 inch (0. 3cm) slices. Cut into flower shape using the mold.

Serves 4—6

1⁄2lb(225g) shrimp (approximately 12 shrimp)

Filling
1⁄2C	ground chicken breast
2T	chopped bamboo shoots
1T	chopped water chestnuts
1⁄2C	cooked crab meat
1⁄8t	salt
1t	rice wine
2t	cornstarch
1⁄2	egg white
12	carrot flowers
	Parsley for garnish

Flatten prawn.

1. Shell prawns, retaining tail. Open each prawn from bottom to form a triangle. Remove vein and flatten prawn.
2. Thoroughly combine filling ingredients. Place a layer of filling on top of each prawn, smoothing top surface with wet fingers.
3. Press a carrot flower on top and place in a heat proof plate.
4. Steam prawns for 15 minutes on medium high heat. Remove and garnish with parsley. Serve with your favorite sauce or dip.

＊Stuffed prawns are delicious coated with batter or *panko* and deep fried. Serve with sweet and sour sauce.

SWEET AND SOUR SAUCE

1½　Cups　Sauce yield

¾C	water
1½T	cornstarch
3T	rice vinegar
3T	catsup
½C	sugar
Dash	of soy sauce

1. Mix together all ingredients in order.
2. Cook and stir until sauce comes to a full boil.
3. Pour into bowl to use with appetizers.

Mix sauce together ahead. Bring to full boil just before serving. Sauce can be kept warm or reheated.

LEMON DIP

yield　½ Cup　sauce

¼C	lemon juice
¼C	soy sauce

1. Mix lemon juice and soy sauce.
2. Pour into bowl to use with appetizers.

Combine filling ingredients throughly.

Place filling on top of each prawn.

Press a carrot flower on top.

Steam prawns for 15 minutes on medium high heat.

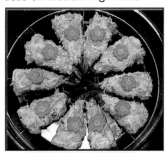

STEAMED CLAMS WITH PORK 豬肉蒸蜆

INGREDIENTS

Serves 4

1½lbs(685g) clams   (approximately 16 clams)
Filling Mixture
½lb(225g)	ground pork
2T	chopped bamboo shoots
2T	chopped water chestnuts
1	black mushroom, soaked, rinsed and chopped
1T	dried cloud ears, soaked, rinsed and chopped
1T each	cornstarch, soy sauce, sesame seed oil
1	green onion, cut in slivers
1T	slivered ginger

Sauce
¼C each	soy sauce, rice vinegar
1T	sesame seed oil

SERVE AS A FIRST COURSE
APPETIZER

1. Soak clams in water with a little salt for 1 hour to remove sand, Clean clams and drain.
2. Place clams in a pot with ½ inch (1.5cm) boiling water. Cover pot and steam for 3 minutes, until clams open shells.
3. Remove clams from shells and set clams aside. Spoon 1 T filling into 1 side of shell. Arrange on a steaming plate, cover and steam for 15 minutes.
4. Return clams to shells and steam 3 minutes more. Garnish with green onions and slivered ginger. Serve with sauce.

① Steam clams until open shells.

② Remove clams and place 1 T filling into shell.

③ Steam for 15 minutes.

④ Return clams to shells and steam 3 minutes more.

CHINESE LONG BEANS WITH SCALLOPS

"SPICED SPARERIBS   (See page   38)",   A GOOD ACCOMPANIMENT   中國長豆角帶子

INGREDIENTS

Serves 4

½lb(225g) scallops
Marinade
1clove   garlic, minced
½t   minced ginger
1t   soy sauce
2t   sesame seed oil
1T   cornstarch

1lb(450g) Chinese long beans

3T   oil

¼C   soup stock
1T   oyster sauce

1.   Make sure scallops are drained well and not wet. Slice into ¼ inch (0.7cm) thick slices. Combine with marinade ingredients.
2.   Pinch off ends of long beans and cut beans into 3 inches (8cm) lengths.
3.   Heat a wok, add 2 T oil. Stir fry scallops approximately 1 minute on high heat, remove and set aside.
4.   Add 1 more T oil to wok and add long beans. Cook for ½ minute and add soup stock. Allow some of soup stock to reduce and add 1 T oyster sauce.
5.   Return scallops to wok and combine.
＊Long beans cook very fast on high heat, do not over cook.
＊If more sauce is desired, add more soup stock and thicken with cornstarch and water.

Combine sliced scallops with marinade.

Stir fry scallops, remove and set aside.

Cook long beans and add soup stock.

After adding oyster sauce, return scallops.

Vegetables & Tofu

垂涎欲滴

Chinese Vegetables

Bamboo shoot : Cream colored, cone shaped shoots of bamboo. Canned shoots are most common. Once opened, store covered with fresh water up to 2 weeks in the refrigerator. Change water once every 4 to 5 days.

Bitter melon : These small melons have a bumpy skin with white flesh. They are oblong and green in color, chartreuse melons have. It has a definite bitter taste. Cut melon in half lengthwise and remove seeds. Cut in thin slices and stir fry with meats.

Bok choy (chinese cabbage or greens) : Dark green leafy vegetable with a white stalk. Keeps in refrigerator for one week.

Cee goo (Arrowhead tubers) : They are egg-size tubes and crisp and starchy.

Coriander or cilantro (Chinese parsley) : A leafy parsley with a pungent flavor. Use as a garnish or may be used to add flavor to most any dish.

Gai Choy (Chinese mustard) : Chinese mustard has pungent-flavored. The leaves resemble bok choy.

Gai lan (Chinese broccoli) : Chinese broccoli has long stalks, topped by small heads of closed buds and the occasional spray of white flowers.

Jit gwa (hairy melon) : Oval shaped, green melon with a fuzzy surface. Peel, slice thin and use in soup.

Leen ngow (lotus root) : The white flesh is pierced by tunnels like the spokes of a wheel.

Water chestnuts : Walnut sized, brown bulb. Must be peeled before use. It is sweet and has a crisp texture similar to apples. Canned water chestnuts are peeled and boiled. They will keep covered with fresh water, in the refrigerator, for about 2 weeks. Change water once a week.

Winter melon : This melon has firm white flesh with mild flavor.

These ingredients are essential to a variety of meatless and almost meatless courses. In addition, they are very economical to buy and high in nutritional content.

CHINESE BROCCOLI WITH OYSTER SAUCE

GOOD ACCOMPANIMENT FOR ANY MEAT DISH

蠔油中國芥蘭

INGREDIENTS

Serves 4

1½lbs(685g)	Chinese broccoli
2T	oil
1clove	garlic, crushed
3T	oyster sauce

How to crush garlic

Using cleaver, press garlic.

1. Clean and rinse broccoli; cut off tough stems.
2. Bring some water to a boil in a large pot. Cook broccoli for 1 minute. Remove and drain.
3. Straighten broccoli, squeeze out excess water and cut into 3 inch (8cm) sections, discarding uneven stems. Place on a serving dish.
4. Heat 2 T oil in wok and fry garlic for ½ minute. Pour oyster sauce and hot oil over broccoli and serve.

Cook broccoli for 1 minute and drain.

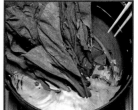

Fry garlic for ½ minute.

Pour oyster sauce and hot oil.

CHICKEN WITH GREENS 鶏片青菜

INGREDIENTS

Serves 4

½lb(225g) tender greens (yu choy)
1T   sesame seed oil

1lb(450g) boneless chicken sliced in ¼ inch (0.7cm) thick slices

Marinade
2T   soy sauce
1T   rice wine
1clove   garlic finely minced
1t   grated fresh ginger root
¼t   sugar
1T   sesame oil
1T   cornstarch

2T   oil

Sauce
½C   chicken stock
1T   soy sauce or oyster sauce
1T   cornstarch

1T   toasted sesame seeds

DELICIOUS ACCOMPANIMENT FOR ANY DISH

1. Remove stems of greens and thoroughly rinse. In a large pot of boiling water blanch greens, drain. Cut greens into 2 inch (5cm) lengths.
2. Toss greens with sesame seed oil and arrange on a platter.
3. Combine chicken with marinade. Heat a wok, add oil and stir fry chicken on high heat until done, about 3 minutes. Reduce temperature if necessary.
4. Add sauce ingredients and bring to a full boil stirring constantly. Allow to cook about ½ minute and serve with greens. Garnish with toasted sesame seeds.

*Bok choy or any other green vegetable may be substituted, but cooking time must be adjusted.

Remove stems and thoroughly rinse.

Cook greens quickly.

Remove and drain.

Cut greens into 2 inch (5cm) lengths.

Toss greens with sesame seed oil.

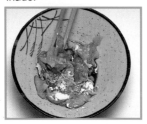

Combine chicken with marinade.

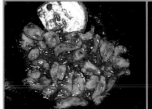

Stir fry chicken. Add sauce ingredients and bring to a full boil stirring constantly.

ASPARAGUS WITH BEEF 梨筍牛肉

EASY ONE DISH MEAL

INGREDIENTS

Serves 4

3/4lb(340g) asparagus (with tough ends removed)

1/4lb(115g) beef sliced 1/4 inch (0.7cm) thick
2t   soy sauce
1/2t   sugar
2t   cornstarch

1T   black beans, rinsed and drained
1clove   garlic, minced
1t   minced ginger
2t   soy sauce

2T   oil

1/2C   soup stock

Cornstarch and water for thickening

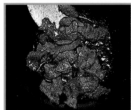
Stir fry beef, remove and set aside.

Combine asparagus with black bean mixture. Add soup stock.

Finally thicken with cornstarch and water.

1. Slice asparagus into 3 inch (8cm) diagonal slices.
2. Combine sliced beef with soy sauce, sugar and cornstarch.
3. Mash black beans with garlic and ginger. Combine with soy sauce.
4. Heat wok, add 1 T oil and stir fry beef until done; remove and set aside.
5. Add 1 T oil to wok and stir fry black bean mixture until fragrant, approximately 1/2 minute. Add asparagus and stir fry to combine with black bean mixture.
6. Add soup stock, cover and cook until crisp tender (approximately 1—2 minutes). Return beef to wok and thicken with cornstarch and water.

STUFFED EGGPLANT

SERVE AS A PART OF DIM
SUM BUFFET

釀 茄

INGREDIENTS

18 pieces

1lb(450g) eggplants

Filling
3/4lb(340g)	shrimp, shelled, devein and chokpped
1/8C	chopped bamboo shoots
1/8C	chopped water chestnuts
1T	soy sauce
1/4t	white pepper
1/2t	sugar
1T	sesame seed oil
1T	cornstarch

Black Bean Mixture
1T	black beans, rinsed
2cloves	garlic, minced
2slices	ginger, minced
1/2t	sugar
3T	oil

Sauce
3/4C	soup stock
1T	cornstarch
2T	soy sauce
1t	sugar
1	green onion, chopped

1. Cut eggplants into 2 inch (5cm) diagonal pieces. Cut a slit in each piece to receive filling ingredients.
2. Combine filling, stuff each piece of eggplant with 1 T of filling.
3. Mash together black bean mixture.
4. Heat skillet, coat with 1 T oil. Slowly pan fry eggplant for 4 minutes on midium high heat. Turn and fry 4 more minutes. Remove and set aside. Continue to cook other pieces in same manner.
5. Heat pan and add black bean mixture, fry for 1/2 minute on medium high heat. Add sauce ingredients, bring to a full boil. Return eggplant to sauce and combine. Garnish with green onions.

Stuff each piece of eggplant with 1 T of filling.

Slowly pan fry eggplant.

After boiling sauce, return eggplant and combine.

SPICY EGGPLANT 五香茄 🌶

DELICIOUS SERVED OVER COOKED NOODLES

INGREDIENTS

Serves 4

½lb(225g)	small eggplants
2T	oil
1T	minced garlic
1T	minced ginger
½lb(225g)	ground pork
1T	hot black bean sauce
2T	soy sauce
1T	rice vinegar
½t	sugar
½C	soup stock
1T	sesame seed oil
¼C	chopped green onions

1. Cut ends off eggplant, dice eggplants into ¾ inch (2cm) cubes.
2. Heat a wok and add oil. Add garlic, ginger and ground pork. Cook until pork turns grey.
3. Add eggplant, black bean sauce, soy sauce, vinegar, sugar and soup stock, Reduce temperature and cook until most of sauce is reduced and eggplant is tender.
4. Add sesame seed oil and chopped green onions.

✳ Adjust hot black bean sauce to taste. Different brands contain various other ingredients allowing for changes in flavor.

Dice egg plants into ¾ inch (2cm) cubes.

Heat wok and add oil. Add garlic and ginger.

Add ground pork and cook.

Add eggplant and sauce ingredients and cook.

SAIFUN WITH VEGETABLES (JAI)

NUTRITIOUS VEGETARIAN DISH

羅漢素齋

INGREDIENTS

All ingredients are assembled.

Soak saifun(page 65), tiger lily buds(page 48), bean curd rolls(page 65), black mushroom(page 100), and cloud ears(page 65). Slice each ingredient if necessary.

Serves 4-6

1/4oz(8g)	bean curd rolls (soaked in hot water; cut into 2 inch/5cm pieces)
2	black mushrooms(soaked, rinsed and sliced)
2T	cloud ears (soaked and rinsed)
1/4C	tiger lily buds (soaked and hard stems removed)

1/2C	sliced lotus root (peeled and sliced 1/4 inch/0.7cm thick)

1T	oil
1clove	garlic, minced
2T	fermented black beans (rinsed and drained)
1/4C	sliced bamboo shoots
1/4C	sliced water chestnuts
1/4C	straw mushrooms

2ozs(60g)	saifun (soaked in hot water until soft, drained)

1—2T	red bean curd (nam yu)
2T	oyster sauce
1T	soy sauce
1C	soup stock

2	green onions cut diagonally into strips

How to soak

Bean curd rolls

Soak in hot water until soft. Rinse and cut into desired size before using.

Saifun

Soak in hot water until soft, drain.

Cloud ears

Soak in warm water 15 minutes to soften. Rinse, remove hard knobs on bottom of ear before using.

Bean curd rolls

Saifun

Cloud ears

1. Simmer bean curd rolls, mushrooms, cloud ears and tiger lily buds for 10 minutes in water or soup stock. Drain and set aside.
2. Heat wok, add oil. Add garlic and black beans; allow mixture to fry for a few seconds.
3. Add all remaining ingredients except bean curd rolls and green onions. Reduce temperature and continue to cook until soup stock is reduced.
4. Mix in bean curd rolls, continue to cook for ½ minute and toss in green onions.

* Increase amount of black beans to taste.

* Tiger lily buds can be tied into knots.

* This is a traditional New Year vegetarian dish.

VEGETABLES

Selection of vegetables is important. Select for balance of flavor, color and texture.

Cutting: Density and size of vegetable determine cutting style and thickness. This in turn determines the cooking time and tenderness.

Fine shredded vegetables require less cooking time and in turn less liquid to complete cooking process.

Denser vegetables such as broccoli, cauliflower and green beans require more liquid and longer cooking time.

Peel lotus root.

Slice lotus root ¼ inch (0.7cm) thick.

Cook all ingredients in order.

THREE MUSHROOM TOFU HOT POT

三菇豆腐煲

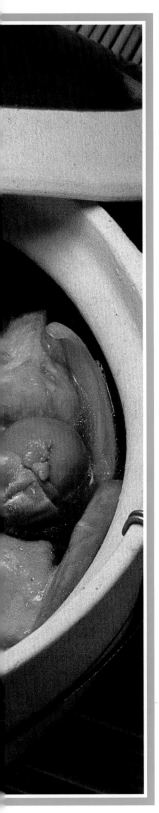

INGREDIENTS

Serves 4—8

Prepare ahead.

1	16oz(450g)cube *tofu*
¼C	cornstarch
3C	oil (375°F/190°C)
2T	oil
1clove	garlic, minced
½C	sliced chicken or pork (cut into ½ inch/ 1.5cm thick slices)
¼C	sliced onions
½C	straw mushrooms
2	black mushrooms, soaked, rinsed and sliced
½C	fresh mushrooms (small bunch, cut lower stems to separate)
¼C	bamboo shoots
1T	rice wine
1T	soy sauce
1T	oyster sauce
½t	salt
¾C	soup stock
1T	cornstarch
2C	*nappa* cut in 2 inch (5cm) pieces

Green onions or carrot flowers for garnish

1. Rinse *tofu,* set on plate and allow to drain for ½ hour or longer to remove excess water. Cut *tofu* into 2 inch (5cm) cubes. Dry cubes with paper towels and dust with cornstarch.
2. Deep fry in hot oil until golden brown. Remove and drain.
3. Heat clean wok and add 2 T oil. Add garlic and meat. Stir fry meat until almost done, add onions and remaining vegetables and seasonings.
4. Combine soup stock with cornstarch. Add to vegetable mixture and bring to a full boil. Return *tofu* to wok and combine.
5. Line the bottom of sandy pot with *nappa.* Pour all ingredients into pot, cover and simmer for 2 minutes. Garnish with green onions.

∗Other vegetables may be used such as bok choy or pea pods.
∗*Tofu* is another word for bean curd.

Dust *tofu* cube with cornstarch.

Deep fry in hot oil.

Pour soup stock and cornstarch.

Return *tofu* to wok.

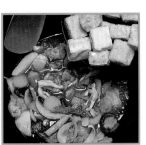

Line the bottom of sandy pot with nappa.

Cover and simmer for 2 minutes.

FRIED TOFU WITH GROUND PORK

GOOD ACCOMPANIMENT FOR ANY DISH

紅燒豆腐豬肉

INGREDIENTS

1	14 oz (400g) cube *tofu*	1/4C	chopped onions
		1T	sweet bean paste
3C	oill for deep frying (350°F / 175℃)	1T	soy sauce
		1/2C	soup stock
		1/2C	green peas
1T	oil		
1clove	garlic, minced		Cornstarch and water for thickening
1t	minced ginger		
1/2lb(225g)	ground pork	1T	sesame seed oil

Tofu squares and chopped onions.

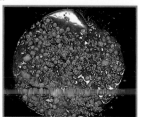

Deep fry *tofu* squares.

1. Remove *tofu* from carton, rinse and allow to drain for 1 hour. Cut into 2 inch (5cm) squares
2. Heat 3 C oil in wok to 350°F (175℃). Deep fry *tofu* squares until golden brown. Remove and set aside.
3. Heat a clean wok and add 1 T oil. Fry garlic and ginger for 1/2 minute. Add ground pork and cook until grey.
4. Add all seasonings, soup stock and peas. Bring to a full boil and thicken with cornstarch mixture.
5. Stir in sesame seed oil and serve mixture over fried *tofu*.

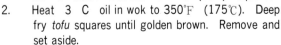

Fry ingredients and thicken.

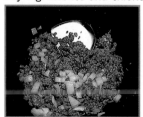

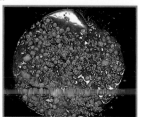

STEAMED STUFFED TOFU

SERVE WITH ANY SPICY DISH

釀豆腐

INGREDIENTS

1	16oz(450g)cube *tofu*
½lb(225g)	boneless white fish fillet
½lb(225g)	shrimp shelled and deveined

Seasoning	
½t	salt
¼t	white pepper
1T	sesame seed oil
1T	rice wine
1t	finely grated ginger
1clove	garlic, minced
1T	cornstarch
½	egg white
1T	finely slivered ginger
2—3T	soy sauce
1T	sesame seed oil
⅛C	slivered green onions

1. Gently rinse *tofu* cubes and place on a plate and allow to drain off excess liquid for several hours.
2. Finely mince fish and shrimp ; combine with seasoning ingredients.
3. Cut *tofu* cube in half lengthwise, then divide each half into 4 pieces. Remove 1 T *tofu* from each piece and stuff with 1 heaping T filling. (Wet fingers to smooth top of filling)
4. Arrange stuffed *tofu* on heat proof plate, sprinkle with ginger and steam for 15 minutes on medium heat.
5. Drain off liquid, pour on soy sauce and sesame seed oil. Garnish with green onions.

* For a spicy taste use hot sesame seed oil.

* Hot black bean sauce is very good as a dip.

Finely mince fish and shrimp.

Combine with seasoning ingredients.

Remove 1 T *tofu*.

Stuff with filling and steam.

Soups 鐘鳴鼎食

The role of soup in a Chinese meal is that of a beverage served throughout the meal, but traditionally towards the end of the meal.

How to make soup stock

yield   6   cups

1	carcass of chicken or 3 cups bones
8C	water
2	slices ginger root
1	scallion

1. Place the bones, ginger, scallion, and the water in a pot and bring to a full boil on high heat.
2. Skim froth and fat, turn temperature to simmer, cover and simmer stock for 1hour.
3. Remove bones and strain soup stock with a fine mesh strainer. Cheesecloth may be used if desired.
4. Skim soup of excess fat. Allow soup to cool, then refrigerate. Fat will harden on the surface and can be easily removed with a strainer.

＊Salt is usually not added until soup stock is used . Soup stock can be used in place of water in most recipes, making the dish more flavorful. Canned chicken broth is a good substitute.

＊Stock may be stored in the refrigerator for up to 5 days. Freeze stock in ice cube trays, then store in plastic bags and use as needed.

＊Use pork bones to make pork soup stock or a combination of pork and chicken bones. Increase water and simmering time for larger bones.

＊The proper proportion of water to bones is just enough water to cover the bones, if enough bones have been accumulated.

＊Use beef stock only for beef dishes.

＊A whole chicken can be used instead of bones. After cooking, reserve chicken for another use.

SOUP VARIATIONS

Soups made with basic soup stocks using either method.. 4 C of soup stock seasoned with salt : (4-6 servings)

1. Winter melon soup
½ lb (225g) winter melon. Remove hard outer skin and seeds. Dice in ½ inch (1.5cm) cubes. Add some diced black forest mushrooms for color and flavor. (Soak and rinse mushrooms first). Bring soup stock to a full boil, add all ingredients, cover and cook slowly for 10 minutes.

2. Hairy melon soup
1 medium melon (about 1½ C sliced). Peel and rinse melon. Slice into ¼ inch (0.7cm) thick slices and cook soup 10 minutes (1"×1"×¼"/2.5×2.5×0.7 cm) slices.

3. *Nappa*, bok choy, pea pod, watercress, spinach. Bring soup stock to a boil and add the desired vegetable, sliced in small pieces, and cook until done (1 or 2 minutes). Vegetables cook very fast. Try to retain green color.

All of the above soups are prepared basically the same way. Vary the ingredients to vary the soup. Use different garnishes such as cooked ham or crab to make soups more elegant. Soups are usually served with the dinner, but to make serving easier, serve soup before the main dishes.

SNOW EAR SOUP 雪耳湯

INGREDIENTS

Serves 4

1C	dried snow ears
½C	thinly sliced chicken breast
1t	soy sauce
1t	sesame seed oil
1t	cornstarch
6C	chicken stock
2	dried forest mushrooms, soaked, rinsed and sliced ¼ inch(0.7cm) thick
¼C	sliced water chestnuts
¼C	sliced bamboo shoots
½C	pea pods or other green vegetables
	Salt to taste
1t	sesame seed oil

GOOD ACCOMPANIMENT FOR ANY MEAL

How to prepare snow ears.

1. Soak snow ears in hot water for 5 minutes. Rinse and remove any hard knobs on bottom of cluster.
2. Combine chicken with soy sauce, sesame seed oil and cornstarch. Bring soup stock to a full boil, add snow ears, mushrooms, water chestnuts and bamboo shoots, cook for 5 minutes.
3. Add chicken and green vegetables, stir to separate chicken, return soup to a full boil and cook 2 minutes.
4. Season with salt to taste, add sesame seed oil and serve.

① Soak in hot water.

② Rinse and remove any hard knobs on bottom of cluster.

After adding chicken and green vegetables, return soup to a full boil and cook 2 minutes.

SIZZLING RICE SOUP 啫啫飯湯

EXCITING BEGINNING FOR ANY MEAL

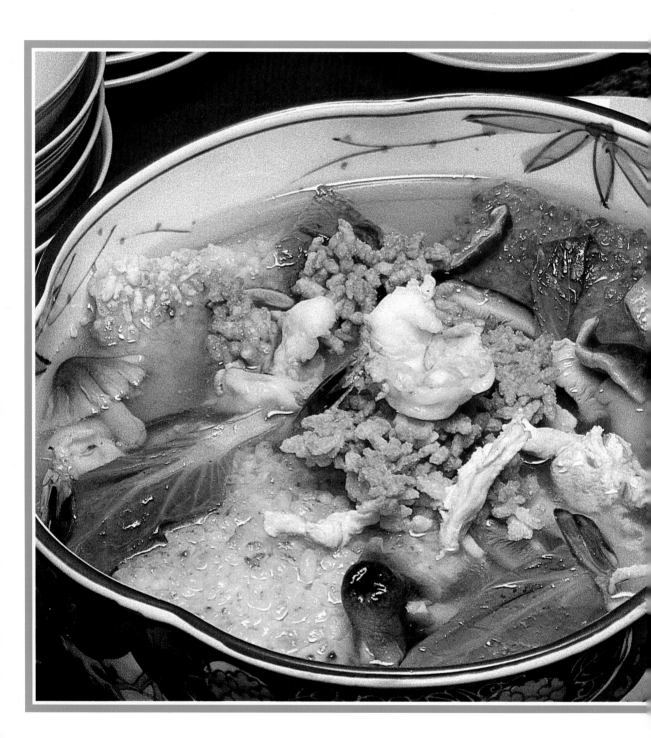

INGREDIENTS

1T	oil
2C	cooked calrose rice (short grain rice) or prepared dried rice squares
1C	thinly sliced chicken breast
2t	rice wine
1/4t	sugar
2t	cornstarch
6C	seasoned chicken stock
1/4lb(115g)	prawns, shelled, deveined and cut in half
2	black mushrooms, soaked, rinsed and sliced thin or straw mushrooms
1C	sliced Chinese greens
2T	rice wine
1t	sesame seed oil
3C	oil (375°F / 190°C) to deep fry rice just before serving

1. Line a baking sheet with foil, lightly oil surface. Press rice onto a baking sheet so the rice cake is ½ inch(1.5cm) thick. Bake at 375°F (190°C) for approximately 45 minutes or until light brown.
2. Remove from oven and allow to cool. Break into smaller pieces and set aside.
3. Combine sliced chicken with wine, sugar and cornstarch.
4. Bring soup stock to a boil, add chicken, prawns, mushrooms, and vegetables. Return soup to a boil and cook 1 minute. Add wine and sesame seed oil.
5. While soup is cooking, deep fry rice pieces until puffed and golden brown.
6. Pour soup in serving bowl and add puffed rice as soon as possible to achieve the loudest sizzling sound possible.

∗Both soup and rice must be hot to create the sizzling sound.
∗Dried rice squares can be purchased. Need only deep frying.

How to make puffed rice.

① Press rice on to a oiled baking sheet ½ inch (1. 5cm) thick and bake.

② Break into smaller pieces, deep fry.

③ Deep fry until puffed and golden brown.

④ When using purchased dried rice squares.

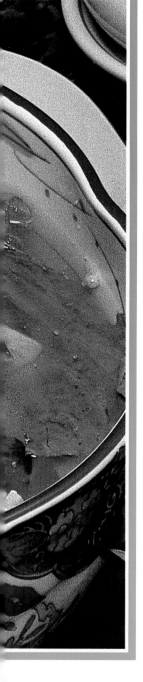

WINTER MELON SOUP 冬瓜盅

INGREDIENTS

IMPRESSIVE SOUP FOR COMPANY DINNER

Serves 4—6

1	small winter melon (approximately 8 1bs 3.600g)
8C	chicken stock
4	large dried black mushrooms, soaked, rinsed and diced
½C	water chestnuts or bamboo shoots
4C	diced winter melon (removed from upper and lower portions of melon)
½C	diced pork
1C	slivered pea pods
1C	cooked crab meat or shrimp meat
½C	diced ham

1. Retain the more attractive portion of winter melon to serve as the bowl. Remove upper $\frac{1}{3}$ of melon.
2. Use the cut portion of melon to make a stand for stability during serving. Remove some of the melon flesh and dice it to put in the soup.
3. Remove seeds and clean out center of melon. Carefully remove $\frac{1}{2}$ inch (1.5cm) of melon from the inside cavity. Trim and dice melon to total approximately 4 C.
4. Clean the outside of melon with damp cloth. Cut attractive border on top of melon. Carve design or words on outside surface of melon.
5. Bring soup stock to a full boil, add mushrooms and diced winter melon. Cover and simmer for approximately 20 minutes.
6. Select a large pot which will hold melon. Fill pot with 2 inches (5cm) of water. Place melon securely on a wok stand. Tie heavy string to holes on stand to make removing melon easier. Or place melon in a large bowl.
7. Lower melon into pot, secure strings and fill melon $\frac{3}{4}$ full with boiling soup. Cover and steam for 15 minutes.
8. Remove soup from melon and put back into previous pot of soup. Carefully remove melon from pot or steamer.
9. Return soup to a boil, add pork and cook for 5 minutes. Add pea pods, shrimp and ham.
10. Serve soup in winter melon bowl.

①Remove upper 1/3 of melon

②Remove seeds and clean out center of melon.

③Dice melon removed from upper and lower portions to total approximately 4 C.

④Carve design or words on outside.

⑤Bring soup stock to a boil, add mushrooms, diced winter melon and water chestnuts (or bamboo shoots).

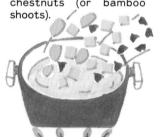

⑥Select a large pot.

⑦Fill pot with 2 inches (5cm) of water. Lower melon into pot, secure strings and fill melon 3/4 full with boiling soup stock.

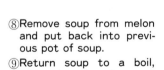

⑧Remove soup from melon and put back into previous pot of soup.
⑨Return soup to a boil, add pork and cook.

⑩Add pea pods, shrimp and ham.

FIRE POT　火　鍋

INGREDIENTS

ELEGANT MEAL FOR COOL WINTER ENTERTAINING

2oz(60g)	bean threads, (soak in hot water until soft)
1/2lb(225g)	shrimp, shelled, deveined and cut in half lengthwise
1/2lb(225g)	beef sliced paper thin or (*sukiyaki* meat)
1/4lb(115g)	chicken breast sliced paper thin
1/2lb(225g)	*tofu* cut into 1 inch (2.5cm) cubes
1/2lb(225g)	firm fish fillet sliced thin or other seafood
1/4lb(115g)	mushrooms sliced
1/4lb(115g)	*nappa* sliced
1small bunch	Chinese parsley, (cilantro)
1bunch	tender spinach leaves
8C	chicken stock
1/4C	rice wine

Sauce A

3T	creamy peanut butter or sesame seed paste
2T	soy sauce
1t	sugar
1T	sesame seed oil
2t	rice vinegar
2t	finely minced ginger
2cloves	finely minced garlic
1	green onion minced

Other sauces

Mix equal amounts of soy sauce with lemon juice
Hot mustard sauce
Hot sesame seed oil
Hot bean sauce with soy sauce

To prepare hot pot

1. Arrange all ingredients on a large platter ; or ingredients may be arranged in separate plates. Prepare sauce A and pour in individual sauce plates.
2. Bring soup stock to a boil and add wine. Pour soup into fire pot and place in center of dining table. Arrange all foods and sauces around pot.
3. Each guest selects meats and vegetables to be cooked and places food in wire baskets to be cooked in fire pot.
4. Dip cooked food in desired sauce before eating.
5. The meal ends with a delicious soup using all remaining ingredients.

How to use fire pot

1) Begin heating charcoal outside in a metal container.
2) When coals are hot, place a layer of coals in base of fire pot.
3) Add heated soup stock to ring pot and place atop coals.
4) Begin meal and add more hot coals as needed.

∗ The fire pot is heated with hot charcoal briquettes. More must be added as needed during meal.

∗ Make sure fire pot is well insulated from table as it gets very hot.

∗ Use this type of fire pot only in a very well ventilated room.

∗ Electric woks can be used as a substitute cooking equipment.

Noodles 山珍海錯

The staple course served in any Chinese meal consists of either rice or noodles.

PORK NOODLES 豬肉麵

INGREDIENTS

½lb(225g) noodles, boiled, rinsed and drained

6C   chicken stock (seasoned with salt to taste)
3C   sliced Chinese greens

16slices   barbecued pork (recipe in Enjoy Chinese Cuisine)[※]
2   hard boiled eggs, quartered

Garnishes
Chopped green onions
Chinese parsley
Sliced salted turnip
Sliced Szechuan preserved vegetable
Assorted ground chili peppers

Meats
Barbecued duck
Roast chicken
Ham
Fried FISH PATTIES (See page 52)

Sauces
Soy sauce with sesame seed oil
Soy sauce with chili oil
Hot mustard and soy sauce
Hot black bean paste
Hot soy bean paste
Any combination of above

※ The title of author's 2nd book

Cook noodle. (10-15 minutes)

Rinse and drain after boiling.

Pour hot soup into bowl before serving.

1.   Bring soup stock to a boil. Add greens and cook just until tender.
2.   Have noodles in individual bowls. Arrange greens, barbecued pork, egg half and green onions on top of noodles. Pour hot soup into bowl.
3.   Serve with assorted condiments and sauces for guests to select.

EASY MEAL FOR BUSY TIMES

*A delicious easy hot meal on cold winter days.
*One large serving bowl can be made instead of individual servings. Guests can serve themselves.

OYSTER SAUCE BEEF NOODLES

蠔油牛肉麵

OTHER VEGETABLES MAY BE USED

INGREDIENTS

Slice ingredients

Serves 4

½lb(225g) Chinese noodles

2T	oil
½lb(225g)	flank steak
1C	sliced fresh mushrooms
¼C	oyster sauce
½C	soup stock
2	green onions cut into 1 inch (2.5cm) pieces

Cornstarch and water for thickening

1. Bring large pot of water to a boil and cook noodles until tender. Rinse, drain and place on a platter.
2. Slice steak into ¼ inch (0.7cm) thick slices against the grain.
3. Heat a wok and add oil. Stir fry beef until done.
4. Push beef up the side of wok and add mushrooms ; stir fry for a few seconds.
5. Add oyster sauce and soup stock, bring to a boil. Add green onions and thicken with cornstarch mixture.
6. Stir in beef and serve over noodles.

＊Use hot oil or chili paste as a dip for noodles.

SPICY PORK NOODLES

五香豬肉麵

SERVE WITH CHICKEN ROLLS

INGREDIENTS

2T	sweet bean sauce
2T	hot soy bean paste
2T	soy sauce
2T	hoisin sauce
1T	sugar
½C	soup stock
½t	salt

Cornstarch and water for thickening

2	green onions chopped

Serves 4

2T	oil
2clove	garlic, minced
1T	minced ginger
1lb(450g)	ground pork
1	onion diced

½lb(225g) noodles, boiled and rinsed in hot water; drained

① Fry garlic and ginger.

② Stir fry pork until grey.

③ Thicken.

④ Serve over noodles.

1. Heat a wok, add oil and fry garlic and ginger for ½ minute.
2. Stir fry pork until grey.
3. Add onion and all seasonings, soup and salt. Bring to a boil and thicken with cornstarch and water.
4. Serve over hot noodles. Toss in green onions.

＊Serve with hot pepper, chili oil, chopped Chinese parsley.

INGREDIENTS

Serves 4

½lb(225g) boneless chicken,
sliced thin

Marinade for chicken
1 clove	garlic, minced
1t	grated ginger
1t	crushed red chili pepper
1T	soy sauce
2t	sesame seed oil
¼t	sugar
1T	rice wine
1T	cornstarch

½lb(225g)	fresh thin egg noodles
¼C	oil

3T	oil
2T	rice wine
2t	hot bean paste
1T	soy sauce

½C	sliced onions
¼C	sliced carrots (cut in favorite design)
1C	sliced fresh mushrooms
1	black mushroom, soaked and sliced
2C	Chinese greens (other colorful assorted vegetables may be used)

½C	chicken stock
¼t	salt or to taste
	Cornstarch and water for thickening

CHICKEN CHOW MEIN WITH THIN NOODLES

鶏炒細絲麵

DELICIOUS AS ONE DISH MEAL

1. Marinate chicken for ½ hour or longer.
2. Cook noodles in plenty of boiling water just until tender, do not over cook. Rinse and drain. Pan fry noodles in a non-stick skillet with ¼ C oil, turning noodles one time to form a golden brown noodle cake. Remove to platter and keep warm.
3. Heat wok, add 2 T oil and stir fry chicken on very high heat until all the meat turns white. Add rice wine, hot bean paste and soy sauce. Allow liquid to reduce. Remove and set aside.
4. Clean wok, heat until hot and add 1 T oil. Stir fry all vegetables, add soup stock and bring to a boil cooking the vegetables quickly. Season with salt and thicken with cornstarch mixture.
5. Serve vegetables over noodle cake and top with hot chicken.

① Cook noodles in plenty of boiling water just until tender. Do not over cook.

② Rinse and drain. Pan fry noodles with ¼ C oil.

③ Stir fry chicken on very high heat and add wine, bean paste, soy sauce.

④ Clean wok. Stir fry all vegetables, add soup stock. Season with salt and thicken with cornstarch mixture.

Boil noodle and rinse in hot water.

Mince shelled shrimp and chop onions finely.

SHRIMP WON TON NOODLE

SERVE WITH A SELECTION OF HOT SAUCES

蝦雲吞麵

1. Combine all filling ingredients and allow to marinate ½ hour.
2. Place 2 t filling in center of wrapper, gently gather wrapper and seal filling with water. Pinch won ton to enclose filling.
3. Bring a large pot of water to a boil and boil won tons for 1 minute. Rinse in cold water and drain.
4. Bring soup stock to a boil and add won tons. Cook 3 minutes adding greens and cooking just until tender.
5. Divide cooked noodles and place into 4 bowls. Ladle won tons and soup over noodles. Serve with garnishes and assorted sauces.

＊After wrapping won tons, deep fry in 350°F (175°C) oil until golden brown. Delicious served with sweet and sour sauce or lemon sauce. Deep fried won tons can be served in soup with noodles and vegetables.

＊Other meats and vegetable may be added to filling.

Serves 4

½lb(225g) thin won ton skins

Filling
1lb(450g)	shrimp (shelled, deveined and minced)
¼C	chopped water chestnuts
¼C	finely chopped onions
1T	sesame seed oil
1T	soy sauce
½t	salt
¼t	sugar
⅛t	white pepper
2T	rice wine
2T	cornstarch

6—8C	seasoned chicken stock

¼lb(115g)	Chinese greens, sliced

½lb(225g)	thin Chinese noodles, boiled and rinse in hot water

Chopped green onions or Chinese parsley

Combine all filling ingredients.

Wrap filling.

Cook won tons.

Add greens.

WIDE NOODLE STIR-FRY

INGREDIENTS

GOOD ACCOMPANIMENT FOR ANY
MEAT DISH

炒潤麵

To prepare ahead.

Serves 4

½lb(225g) wide or thick noodles

½lb(225g)	boneless meat, sliced thin
1t	grated fresh ginger
2cloves	garlic, minced
1T	soy sauce
1T	cornstarch
2T	oil
½C	sliced onions
½C	slivered carrots
4C	sliced cabbage (½ inch/1.5cm wide slices)
½C	sliced fresh mushrooms
1C	sliced green or red peppers or broccoli
½C	pea pods
¼C	soy sauce
1T	rice wine
1T	rice vinegar
2T	sesame seed oil
½t	salt
½t	pepper

1. Bring a large pot of water to a boil, add noodles ; stir to separate reducing temperature. Cook noodles just until tender. Rinse and drain noodles ; set aside.
2. Combine meat with ginger, garlic, soy sauce and cornstarch.
3. Heat a wok, add oil and stir fry meat until done. Remove and set aside.
4. Add all vegetables and stir fry 2—3 minutes. Reduce temperature, add noodles and all seasonings. Return meat to wok and combine.

* Other noodles and vegetables may be substituted.

* Japanese *tonkatsu* sauce can be used instead of soy sauce.

Prepare noodles.

① Stir fry meat, remove and set aside.

② Stir fry all vegetables 2—3 minutes.

③ Add noodles and all seasonings. Return meat.

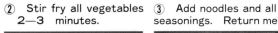

SPICY COLD NOODLES

五香凍麵

SERVE WITH "FISH PATTIES" (See page 52)

INGREDIENTS

Serves 4

1/4lb(115g) Chinese noodles

1T   Szechuan peppercorns

1C   shredded barbecued pork
1C   shredded cooked chicken breast
1C   shredded seedless cucumber
1   green onions chopped

Sauce
1/4C   peanut butter
3T   soy sauce
1T   sugar
1T   chili oil
2T   sesame seed oil
1T   minced garlic
1T   minced ginger
1/4C   rice vinegar

1. Boil noodles until tender. Rinse in cold water, drain and set aside in serving dish.
2. Lightly toast peppercorns in skillet, grind and strain to remove hard bits of shell. Set aside.
3. Arrange chicken, cucumbers and green onions on top of noodles.
4. Combine sauce and serve with noodles. Serve with pepper along side.

Boil noodles until tender.

Rinse in cold water, drain.

How to prepare peppercorns

Lightly toast peppercorns in skillet.

Grind.

Strain to remove hard bits of shell.

Sliver pork and cucumber. Chop onion.

Combine sauce ingredients.

How to make barbecued pork

2 ½—3lbs(685—1.350g) boneless pork (pork loin or tenderloin) cut into 2½×2×7 inch (4×5×18cm) pieces

Marinade

1½t	salt
1T	rice wine
½t	garlic powder
2T	hoisin sauce
¼C	catsup
¼C	sugar
3	drops red food coloring (optional) paper clips to hang pork strips

1. Marinate pork strips at least 2 hours or overnight in the refrigerator.
2. Place roast on a rack over some water in a roasting pan. Bake at 350°F (175°C) for 1 hour or until done. Be sure to turn pork at least once. Allow to cool.

Marinate

Roast on a rack over a pan of water

How to prepare cooked chicken breast

1	chicken breast
1t	salt
5T	rice wine.
½	green onion, chopped (optional)
1T	crushed ginger (optional)

1. Clean chicken breast and dry with paper towels.
2. Rub chicken with salt to tighten. Rinse chicken well.
3. Place chicken in a pot and pour in enough water to cover chicken. Add wine, green onion and ginger.
4. Bring to a boil and simmer for approximately 45 minutes.
5. Allow to cool.
6. Remove chicken meat from bones. Hit meat with cleaver and the meat will be easier to shred.

Simmer

Slice

Shred

STEAMED NOODLES 腸 粉

USE AS A NOODLE IN ANY RECIPE

INGREDIENTS

5-6 rolls

1C	cake flour, sifted
2T	cornstarch
½t	salt
1T	oil
1¼C	water

1. Combine all ingredients thoroughly, making sure there are no lumps. Use a blender if possible. Strain mixture if lumps are present.
2. Prepare the wok for steaming with a rack to hold an 8 or 9 inch (20 or 23cm) round cake pan.
3. Oil pan and place on rack in wok. Pour in about ⅓ C of batter just to cover bottom of pan.
4. Cover, and steam on high heat for 5 minutes. Remove pan from steamer and float pan in some cold water. Allow to cool.
5. Remove noodle from pan by rolling (jelly roll style).
6. Clean pan if necessary and repeat process until all of batter is used. Use several pans to make this process easier and faster.
7. Slice noodles into ¾ inch (2cm) wide pieces.
   Use these noodles for Chow Fun, or other stir fried dishes which can be served with noodles.

Combine all ingredients.

Pour batter in oiled pan.

Cover, and steam.

Roll noodle.

＊This recipe is much easier to make than rice noodles. Rice flour can be used instead of cake flour. Be sure to thoroughly steam rice noodles or they will be very sticky.

＊Many fillings can be added to noodles before steaming and then rolled and served with a variety of sauces or dips.

＊Sauce
   2T soy sauce
   1T sesame seed oil
   ?t hot bean paste

See recipe overleaf

STEAMED NOODLES WITH FILLING

SERVE AS PART OF DIM SUM BUFFET

有餡腸粉

Prepare : One recipe of **STEAMED NOODLES** batter (See page86)

One recipe pork and Sausage Filling (See below)

OR

One recipe of Shrimp Filling (See below)

Shown on page   87

STEAMED NOODLES WITH FILLING

Scatter pork and sausage over surface of noodle.

Roll noodle jelly roll style.

Pork and Sausage

1. Prepare one recipe of noodle batter for every 5 or 6 rolls.
2. Oil pan and place on rack in steamer.
3. Pour ⅓ C batter into pan to coat bottom of pan. Scatter Pork and Sausage Filling over surface of noodle.   Cover and steam for 5 minutes on high heat.
4. Remove pan and cool. Roll noodle jelly roll style and cut in half before serving. Serve with assorted sauces.

Place shrimp.

Roll noodle.

Shrimp

1. Place Shrimp Filling on lower ⅓ of batter. Steam and cool as directed.
2. Roll noodle, cut in half and serve with assorted sauces.

∗Filled noodles are delicious with soy sauce, sesame seed oil and hot bean paste as dips.

PORK AND SAUSAGE FILLING   豬肉臘腸腸粉

Prepared ingredients

1T	oil
1C	ground pork
2	Chinese sausages, finely chopped
2	black mushrooms, soaked, chopped
¼	chopped shrimp meat
2T	chopped salted turnip
½C	chopped onions
1Teach	soy sauce, rice wine, sesame seed oil
	Chopped green onions for garnish

1. Heat wok until hot, add oil. Stir fry pork until grey,   add sausage.   Add all other ingredients and stir fry until liquid is reduced.
2. Toss in green onions.   Use as a filling for steamed noodles.

∗Dried shrimp,   chopped water chestnuts and other ingredients can be added.
∗This filling is delicious as stuffing for steamed SHRIMP AND PORK DUMPLINGS(see   page 10). Pleat edge to create a different shape.

SHRIMP FILLING   蝦腸粉

½lb(225g)	shrimp
1T	rice wine
½t	salt
¼t	sugar
2t	sesame seed oil
1T	cornstarch

1. Shell and devein shrimp. Rinse and pat dry with paper towels. Chop shrimp.
2. Combine with remaining ingredients and set aside to be used as a filling for steamed noodle rolls.

∗Other vegetables and meats can be used for fillings. Combinations of shredded meats and vegetables are unlimited. Be creative.

STEAMED NOODLES WITH BLACK BEAN SAUCE

VERY GOOD AS ONE DISH MEAL

豆豉腸粉

INGREDIENTS

Serves 4

1 recipe of **STEAMED NOODLES** (page 86)

3T   oil

½lb(225g) beef sliced thin against the grain

Marinade
1t	minced ginger
1clove	garlic, minced
½t	sugar
1T	soy sauce
1T	cornstarch

Black Bean Mixture
2T	black beans, rinsed
1clove	garlic
1slice	ginger
½t	sugar
½t	crushed red chili pepper
1	small onion, sliced
½	sliced green pepper
½	sliced red pepper
2	black mushrooms, soaked and sliced
1C	choy sum (tender centers of bok choy)
1T	each rice wine, soy sauce
	Salt to taste
½C	soup stock

Cornstarch and water for thickening

1. Have one recipe of STEAMED NOODLES prepared (see page 86) and cut into ¾ inch (2cm) pieces.
2. Combine sliced beef with marinade. Mash black beans with garlic, ginger, sugar and chili pepper, set aside.
3. Heat a non-stick skillet, add 1 T oil and slowly fry noodles until hot. Set aside.
4. Heat wok until hot, add 1 T oil, cook beef, remove and set aside. Add 1 T oil to wok and fry black bean mixture for ½ minute taking care not to burn mixture.
5. Add all vegetables, seasonings and soup stock. Bring to a boil, cook 1 minute and add beef. Thicken with cornstarch mixture.
6. Serve over hot noodles. (Noodles can also be mixed with vegetables)

∗Other stir fried dishes can be cooked with STEAMED NOODLES.

Prepare steamed noodles (See recipe, page 86)

Slowly fry noodles. Set aside.

Cook beef, remove and set aside.

Fry vegetables.

Add beef. Thicken.

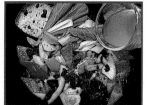

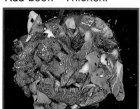

SERVE AS AN APPETIZER FOR
LARGE PARTIES

炸鍋貼檸檬糊

INGREDIENTS

Makes 25

½lb(225g) round noodle wrappers (*gyoza* or
shu mai)

Filling
½lb(225g)	ground pork
¼lb(115g)	prawns, shelld deveined and min-ced
¼C	chopped onions
2T	chopped bamboo shoots
2	black mushrooms, soaked and minced
2C	chopped cabbage
1T	grated ginger
2cloves	garlic, finely min-ced
2T	soy sauce
2T	rice wine
2T	sesame seed oil
½t	salt
2T	cornstarch
3C	oil for deep frying (350°F/175°C)

Lemon Sauce
⅓C	fresh lemon juice
½C	water
1½T	cornstarch
⅓C	sugar
1t	soy sauce
½t	crushed chili pep-per

Sweet and Sour Sauce
⅔C	water
¼C	rice vinegar
1½T	cornstarch
3T	catsup
½C	sugar
2t	soy sauce

1   Combine filling ingredients and allow to marinate ½ hour.
2.   Place 1 T filling in center of wrapper. Wet outer edge of wrapper and close off filling forming a crescent. Hold top edge and press down to flatten bottom. Dumplings may be pleated if desired.
3.   Deep fry in oil for 2—3 minutes or until golden brown. Make sure oil is not too hot.
4.   Prepare lemon sauce or sweet and sour sauce. Serve as dip for POT STICKERS.

Wrap filling.

Deep fry until golden. Make sure oil is not too hot.

Combine all ingredients for each sauce and bring to a full boil stirring constantly.

POT STICKERS WITH CHICKEN AND VEGETABLES

TRY OTHER FILLINGS FOR VARIATIONS

鶏肉蔬菜鍋貼

INGREDIENTS

Serves 4—8

＊**POT STICKER** recipe from page 90

½lb   round noodle wrappers (*gyoza or shu mai*)

Filling
½lb(225g) ground pork
¼lb(115g) prawns, shelled deveined and minced
¼C   chopped onions
2T   chopped bamboo shoots
2   black mushrooms, soaked and minced
2C   chopped cabbage
1T   grated ginger
2cloves garlic, finely minced
2T   soy sauce
2T   rice wine
2T   sesame seed oil
½t   salt
2T   cornstarch

3C   oil for deep frying (350°F／175°C)

＊ ＊ ＊ ＊ ＊ ＊ ＊ ＊ ＊ ＊ ＊ ＊ ＊ ＊

2T   oil
¼lb(115g) boneless chicken sliced thin
¼lb(115g) prawns, shelled, deveined and cut in half
2C   sliced assorted vegetables (carrot flowers)

½C   soup stock
1T   oyster sauce
1T   rice wine

    Cornstarch and water for thickening

1. Prepare POT STICKERS and deep fry following instructions on page 90.
2. Heat wok, add oil and stir fry chicken until done. Add all vegetables, soup stock and seasonings. Bring to a boil, add deep fried pot stickers; cover and cook 1 minute.
3. Thicken with cornstarch and water. Serve with assorted sauces.

＊Barbecued pork and other seafood can be added to stir fry recipe.
＊Deep fried won tons can be substituted for POT STICKERS.

Slice chicken thinly

Stir fry vegetables, soup stock and seasoning.
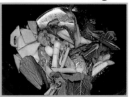

Add fried pot stickers.
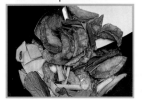

Thicken.

Prepare pot stickers and deep fry following instructions on page 90.

Rice 熟能生巧

The staple course served in any Chinese meal consists of either rice or noodles.

RICE WRAPPED IN LOTUS LEAF

荷葉飯

DELICIOUS AS A COMPLETE MEAL

INGREDIENTS

Soak lotus leaves in hot water and thoroughly rinse. Pat dry.

Makes 6

6	lotus leaves
½lb(225g)	boneless chicken, diced in 1 inch(1.5cm) cubes

Marinade for chicken

½t	grated ginger
2t	soy sauce
2t	sesame seed oil
½t	sugar
1T	cornstarch
4C	**STEAMED GLUTINOUS RICE** (See page 96) or mixture of long grain and short grain rice
1T	oil
1C	diced barbecued pork
2	Chinese sausages, diced
2	black mushrooms, soaked and diced
2T	soy sauce
3T	oyster sauce
2	hard boiled eggs, quartered
½C	Chinese parsley

1. Soak lotus leaves in hot water and thoroughly rinse. Pat dry.
2. Combine chicken with marinade, set aside. Have rice hot and ready. Heat wok, add oil and stir fry chicken until meat is white. Add pork, sausage, mushooms, soy sauce and oyster sauce.
3. Turn off heat and thoroughly mix in rice. Divide rice into 6 equal portions.
4. Place ½ of portion of rice on top side of leaf. Put 1 piece of egg in center and cover with parsley. Cover with remaining portion of rice. Fold bottom of leaf up to cover rice, bring in sides and roll up to enclose contents. Continue with other packets.
5. Place wrapped rice in steamer and steam for 20 minutes.

٭Larger packets can be made if desired adjusting steaming time

Prepare rice filling.

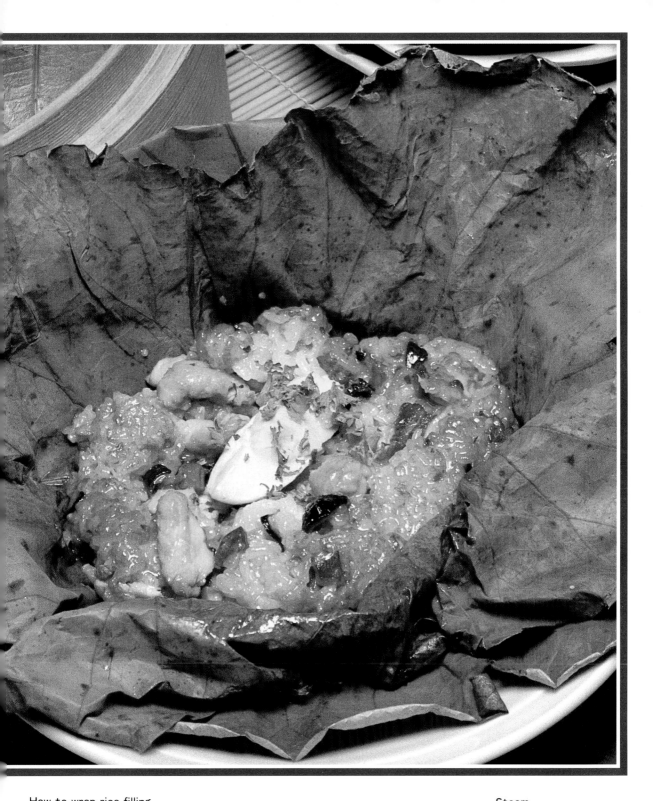

How to wrap rice filling

 → → →

Steam

JEWELED RICE 五彩八寶飯

INGREDIENTS

Chop or dice ingredients.

Serves 4

2T	oil
2	Chinese sausages, diced
½C	diced barbecued pork
2	dried black mushrooms, soaked and diced
½C	diced onions
½C	diced cooked carrots
2T	soy sauce
2T	oyster sauce
1T	sesame seed oil
4C	calrose rice, cooked according to instructions (See page 96)
¼C	chopped green onions or Chinese parsley

＊This recipe is delicious as a stuffing for

1. Heat wok, add 2 T oil. Stir fry sausage for ½ minute and add barbecued pork. Add remaining vegetables.
2. Add seasonings and rice. Continue to fry reducing temperature until rice is hot. Toss in green onions or parsley.

Stir fry and season.

HAM FRIED RICE 火腿炒飯

INGREDIENTS

Serves 4

1T	oil
2	eggs, beaten
2T	oil
1C	diced ham
½C	diced onions
½C	diced red pepper
½C	diced green pepper or Chinese pea pods
4C	cooked rice (long or short grain may be used)
3–4T	soy sauce (may substitute oyster sauce)
	Salt to taste
¼C	chopped green onions

1. Heat a skillet, add 1 T oil. Pour in a thin layer of beaten egg and cook as a thin sheet. Remove and cook remainder of egg in same manner. Allow to cool and cut into thin shreds. Set aside.
2. Heat wok, add 2 T oil, stir fry ham, onions and peppers for ½ minute. Add rice and continue to stir fry until rice is hot reducing temperature if necessary.
3. Add soy sauce and thoroughly combine.
4. Garnish with green onions and eggs. Garnish with extra shredded ham if desired.

✳Use other meats such as barbecued pork, Chinese sausage and chicken. Various meats or vegetables may be added or substituted.

To make shredded egg for garnish.

Step 1

Step 2

Stir fry diced ingredients.

Add soy sauce

STEAMED GLUTINOUS RICE

USE IN FILLING RECIPES

糯米飯

INGREDIENTS

Steam for 40 minutes.

Makes 4 cups

2C glutinous rice

1. Rinse rice until water runs clear. Allow rice to soak in water for 2 hours ; drain.
2. Place a cloth in a steaming rack, spread rice out to an even layer. Make hole in center of rice. Cover steamer ; bring water to a full boil and reduce temperature to medium high. Steam for 40 minutes.

Rice is an integral part of every meal, and is the staple food of China.
Basically, there are three types: long grain, short grain, and glutinous, or sweet rice. Long grain rice is firmer, and is used for fried rice. Short grain is starchier and softer. Japanese *sushi* requires use of short grain rice. Sweet rice is usually used for desserts or stuffings.

STEAMED WHITE RICE

yield 3 cups

yield 4 cups

1C	rice (long grain)	1½C	rice (short grain)
1½C	water	1¾C	water

1. Wash rice by rubbing between hands. (Some brands require no washing.) Drain and repeat until water is clear.
2. Add water, cover saucepan and bring to boil.
3. When rice comes to boil, uncover and allow rice to boil until (75%) or most of liquid evaporates and holes form on surface of rice. Cover rice, allow to steam on very low heat for 20 minutes.
4. Turn heat off and allow rice to sit 5 minutes on burner.
5. Fluff rice before serving.

∗ Water proportion changes as more rice is used. If cooking more rice, add enough water to cover rice 1 inch (1.5cm) or water level should be up to first joint of index finger. Increase or decrease water to the firmness desired.

∗ When cooking short grain rice, use a little less water.

∗ Leftover rice may be refrigerated. Reheat by steaming or use for fried rice.

INFORMATION

COOKING METHODS

The most common Chinese cooking methods include stir-frying, deep-frying, roasting, and steaming. Depending upon the method utilized, ingredients generally retain their natural flavor and nutrition with new and different tastes emerging from the use of each method.

Stir-Frying

This method of cooking combines the elements of high heat and quick, constant tossing to seal in the flavor and juices of meats and vegetables. Stir-frying cooks protein foods thoroughly at the same time leaving them tender and juicy. Vegetables stir-fried until barely tender retain their natural color and crisp texture.

Only a small amount of oil is necessary. Timing and temperature will vary according to the type of pan selected and whether a gas or electric range is used. A flat-bottomed pan or wok which has contact with the heating element will get much hotter than a round-bottomed one. In addition, a gas range is more convenient since you can turn the heat up or down instantly. A good stir-frying temperature is 375 degrees Fahrenheit. If the temperature is too high, the food will burn in which case a lower temperature adjustment is in order. On the other hand, if the temperature is too low, ingredients do not fry, but seep in the oil and will lose their flavor. Therefore, to maintain the proper temperature, constant adjustment of the temperature may be necessary.

Actual stir-frying involves vigorous arm action in the constant stirring and tossing of the food. It is a loud and noisy operation when the food meets the pan and the stirring begins. Actual cooking time will seldom exceed several minutes.

Follow the steps below for effective stir-frying:
1) Heat the wok until it gets hot and add oil (usually 2 tablespoons).
2) Roll the oil around to cover the cooking surface of the wok.
3) When the oil begins to form a light haze, you are ready to add the ingredients.
4) Follow the recipe and remember to adjust the temperature control for the proper stir-frying temperature.

Cornstarch for thickening

Sauces or gravies can be thickened with a variety of starches such as arrowroot, potato, tapioca, or cornstarch. All of these starches produce a translucent gravy, whereas flour will produce an opaque gravy. In Chinese cooking, cornstarch is most often used.

Many recipes call for cornstarch for thickening, but sometimes an exact amount is not given. Mix equal amounts of cornstarch to cold water and stir until cornstarch is dissolved. Usually one tablespoon of cornstarch dissolved in one tablespoon of cold water will be enough to thicken ½ cup of sauce to produce a medium thick gravy.

To thicken a sauce, always push all ingredients to the side of the wok, making a well at the bottom of the wok. Stir cornstarch mixture and pour a small amount into the well. Stir the sauce constatly to prevent lumps. Allow the sauce to come to a boil and see how thick it is. If not thick enough, add more cornstarch mixture until desired thickness is obtained. Always remember to stir the sauce constantly to prevent lumps from forming. When desired thickness is obtained, mix ingredients together gently to coat with sauce.

Deep-frying

Deep-frying requires a large amount of oil in the wok, usually not more than 3-4 cups. A fourteen inch wok is best suited for deep frying. As with stir frying, timing and temperature for deep frying will vary depending upon whether a gas or electric stove is used. Thus, the time given for most recipes is only approximate and adjustments should be made accordingly. Added caution should be exercised whenever oil is used at high temperatures. Never leave the hot oil unattended !

The proper temperature for deep-frying is generally 375 degrees Fahrenheit. The oil should reach this temperature before any ingredients are added. At a temperature of 375 degrees Fahrenheit, the oil will just barely begin to smoke. An easy way to tell whether the oil has reached the desired temperature is to add a drop of batter into the oil. If the drop of batter sinks and slowly returns to the surface, the oil is not yet hot enough. If the batter drops to the bottom and immediately bounces up to the surface, the oil is ready for deep-frying. If the oil smokes, it has gotten too hot and the temperature should be lowered.

The oil used for deep-frying can be saved and used again. To grant your oil longer life, remove food crumbs with the fine mesh strainer during deep-frying. The quality of used oil is judged by its clarity, not by the number of times used nor the length of time used. Fresh oil is light yellow in color and clear. If the used oil is still relatively clear, it is salvageable and readily usable again. However, used oil which appears darker and clouded should be discarded because the temperature at which it will begin to smoke will drop and consequently, a high enough temperature cannot be achieved for proper deep-frying resulting in foods turning out very greasy.

To store the used oil, first strain with a fine mesh strainer. Then place the oil in a heatproof container if the oil is still hot. Allow the oil to cool, cover, and store in the refrigerator until ready to use again. Peanut oil or a good vegetable oil such as corn oil will have a longer usable life as well as possess qualities superior to other oils for purposes of deep-frying foods. None of the pure vegetable oils contain cholesterol and the use of a polyunsaturated oil is strongly recommended.

Follow the steps below for effective deep-frying:
1) Heat 3-4 cups of oil in the wok until a light haze forms at approximately 375 degrees Fahrenheit.
2) Drop in foods and deep-fry until foods are cooked.
3) Adjust the temperature to maintain a constant frying temperature of 375 degrees Fahrenheit. Begin by setting temperature on high; if the oil gets too hot (smokes), turn down temperature to medium high and back to high if the oil drops below 375 degrees Fahrenheit.
4) Follow the instructions given in the recipe.

Roasting, Baking, or Broiling

These cooking methods are so common and ordinary as to require limited explanation.

Meats or rolls may be roasted or baked in the oven. When roasting meats, use a broiling pan or place a rack on the bottom of a pan to support the meat. Add a small amount of water to the bottom of the pan, making sure the meat is above the water level. The water will keep the meat moist and also keep the drippings from burning onto the broiling pan.

Follow the steps below for effective roasting, baking or broiling:
1) Preheat the oven to the required temperature.
2) Place all foods in the center of the oven to allow for even roasting.
3) Follow the instructions given in the recipe.

Steaming

Steaming is one of the most nutritious, not to mention convenient, methods of cooking foods, retaining more nutrients and natural flavor than other conventional means of cooking. Steamed foods seal in natural juices of meats and vegetables which are delicious served over rice.

There are many different types of steamers available. The wok with a cover will serve as a good steamer. Multi-tiered bamboo steamers may be purchased. However, a large pot with a cover will suffice for the purpose of steaming food.

Continued on page 100

Steaming racks are required to support and elevate the plate or bowl which contains food to be steamed in a wok. A round cake rack will serve just as well as commercially available steaming racks. You may even improvise, using a water chestnut can with both ends removed as a substitute for a steaming rack. The rack should be set in the center of the wok or pan.

Three to four cups of water should be sufficient for steaming with a wok and cover. The water level should be about one inch below the steaming rack. Cover the wok and bring the water to a full boil using the highest temperature setting on your stove (full steam). Place the plate or bowl containing the food atop the steaming rack. Make sure the boiling water does not flow over into the bowl or plate. If this does occur, reduce the water level under the steaming rack. After inserting the food, cover and bring water again to a full boil and turn the temperature down to medium high to maintain a constant flow or steam. Be sure there is enough room for the steam to circulate.

All steamers operate according to the same basic principle. The efficient circulation of steam is of paramount importance. Bamboo steamers have several tiers in which many dishes can be steamed simultaneously. The tiers and cover are set on top of a wok containing boiling water. There are also metal steamers consisting of a pot to hold the water and usually two tiers and a cover. For example, the bottom pot functions to cook soup stock while the two tiers are used to steam two other separate dishes. In this manner, many dishes may be steamed at one time saving both time and energy.

Follow the steps below for effective steaming.
1) Pour water in the wok or pot so that the water level stands one inch below the steaming rack or dish of food.
2) Cover the wok and bring the water to a full boil.
3) Use heatproof dishes only for steaming.
4) Insert the dish of food atop the steaming rack. Cover and bring to a full boil (or full steam) again. Turn the temperature down to medium high and allow to steam for the specified time.
5) Check the water level when longer steaming times are necessary.
6) Follow the instructions given in the recipe.

CUTTING METHODS

In Chinese cooking, all ingredients are cut into bite-size morsels before cooking or serving. This is done for aesthetic as well as functional reasons. Vegetables are more appealing with uniform slicing and chopping while ingredients cut the same size and shape cook more evenly and quickly. The following describes the various cutting techniques used in this book.

Slice
Refers to meats or vegetables cut into thin uniform strips usually 2inch(5cm) long by 3/4 -1inch(2-2.5cm) wide and about 1/8 inch(0.3cm) thick or as directed by the recipe.

Sliver or Shred
Refers to meats or vegetables cut 2inch(5cm) long by 1/8inch(0.3cm) wide by 1/8inch(0.3cm) thick to resemble match-sticks or beansprouts.

Dice
To cut into 1/2inch(1.5cm) cubes.

Chop or Mince
To cut into small pieces as in ground beef.

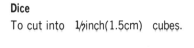

Boning a chicken

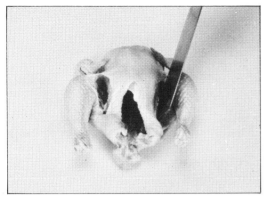

1. Place the chicken on a cutting board, breast side up. With a sharp knife, slice through the skin between the thigh and lower breast, exposing the thigh.

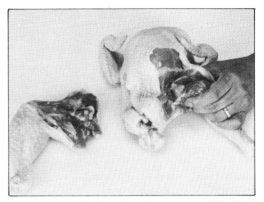

2. Bend the thigh back and carve around the joint to remove the thigh and leg. Remove as much meat as possible from the back of the chicken while removing the thigh and leg. Repeat with the other side in the same manner.

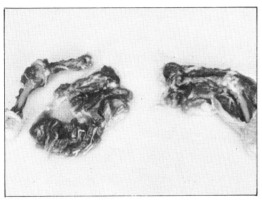

3. To remove meat from leg and thigh : Cut along the inside of the leg and thigh, exposing the bones. Cut the meat away from the thigh bone, separate the joint, and remove the thigh bone. Remove the rest of the meat from the leg bone. Repeat with the other leg and thigh.

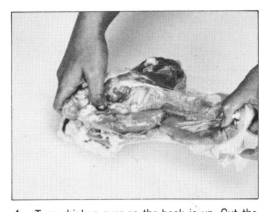

4. Turn chicken over so the back is up. Cut the wings from the back to expose the joint, taking as much meat as possible from the back. Separate at the joint and pull to remove breast meat. This will leave a small piece of chicken (tenderloin) still attached to the breast bone, which should be cut out. Repeat with the other wing in the same manner.

5. Trim off as much meat from the carcass as possible. Use the bones to make soup stock.

How to bone a chicken breast

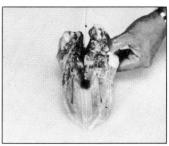

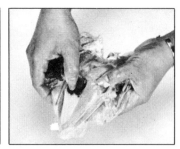

1. Place chicken breast skin side down on a cutting board. Cut ½ inch(1.5cm) into the top of the chicken breast, breaking the white triangular piece of cartilage.

2. Holding the chicken breast with both hands, bend it back to expose the breast bone. The bone should pop up.

3. Run thumb down the breast bone and cartilage.

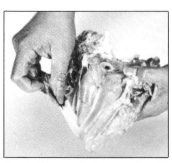

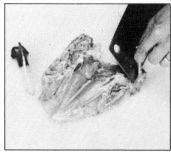

4. Pull the entire bone and cartilage out.

5. Locate the wishbone at the top of the breast, which broke into two pieces when the breast was bent back. Using a sharp knife, cut as much meat from the wishbone as possible.

6. Release meat from the ribs, scraping the bones as you cut. Repeat with the other side of the chicken breast.

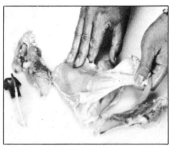

8. Remove the tendons on the underside of the breast. There is one on each side. Now you have a boneless chicken breast. Use as directed in a recipe.

7. Pull skin off and cut off the fat at the bottom of the breast.

Carving a chicken

1. Remove wings, legs and thighs ; set aside.
2. Separate breast from the back ; set breast aside.
3. First, cut the back into bite-sized pieces(1½ × 2inch, 4 × 5cm) and arrange on the center of a platter.
4. Separate wings at the joints, discard tips and place wings pieces on the sides of the upper half of the platter.
5. Cut each thigh in half and place on platter. Place the legs on the sides of the lower half of the platter.
6. Cut breast into bite-sized pieces and place on top of back pieces.
7. Garnish with parsley.

This method of carving can also be used to cut a chicken in preparation for cooking.

UTENSILS

Wok

The Chinese wok is a round or flat-bottomed pan made of heavy gauge carbon steel. It comes in various sizes, but the most functional for our purposes is the 14 inch (35cm) wok. The round-bottomed wok is usually accompanied by a ventilated ring which serves to support the base of the wok above a gas-range burner. A flat-bottomed wok, which dose not require a ring stand, sits atop an electric range, but requires some adjustments during cooking as there is direct contact with the burner, resulting in much hotter temperatures.

When using a gas range, the ring should be situated with the sides slanting downwards and the smaller opening supporting the wok. The round-buttom design of the wok directs the heat source to the center of the wok which gets hot very quickly. The heat is then conducted rapidly and evenly throughout the rest of the wok. When using an electric range, the ring should be placed securely over the burner, with the sides slanting upwards to allow the center of the wok closer proximity to the burner.

Seasoning wok

Scrub the wok in hot sudsy water to remove the protective oil applied when manufactured. Rinse well and dry thoroughly. Season the cleaned wok by heating and rubbing a small amount of peanut oil on the inside surface with a paper towel. Re-heat the wok until hot and repeat the process two more times. Your wok is now ready for use.

During the course of cooking a meal, the wok need only be cleaned with hot water, using a bristle scrub brush used for non-stick pans. When you are through using the wok, wash in sudsy water and rinse. Dry over medium heat and rub a dab of oil on the inside surface to prevent rust. Eventually, with constant use, your wok will assume a darker color on the inside which results in smooth non-stick cooking. Never scour your wok with harsh cleansers. If rust appears, simply scrub clean and reseason. Any time the wok is used for steaming, it must be reseasoned afterward in order afterwards prevent foods from sticking. However, only one coating of oil is necessary for reseasoning your wok.

Electric woks are good substitutes. They are espeically suited for entertaining or cooking at the table. Just follow the package instructions for use and care.

Wok Accessories

Accessories specially designed for wok cooking are avaiable in any cookware store. They greatly facilitate cooking with a wok.

Cover

The size of the dome-shaped cover depends largely upon the diameter of the wok. Sometimes a 10-12inch(25-30cm) cover to a frying pan may suffice. The convenience of a cover is readily apparent when it is necessary to steam ingredients using the wok.

Continued on page 104

Continued from page 103

Curved Spatula

This utensil comes with a long handle with a wide, curved edge which fits the curved bottom of the wok. Ingredients can be more readily tossed and removed using a curved rather than straight-edged spatula.

Draining Rack

This wire semicircular rack attaches to the top of the wok. It is used in deep-frying to drain the oil from the food before removing onto a serving dish.

Wire Strainer, Fine Mesh Strainer

This strainer is made of wire with a long wooden handle. The large holes allow the ingredients to be removed quickly from hot oil, leaving the crumbs or bits of batter behind to be removed by a fine mesh strainer. It is also useful in removing large pieces of foods from soups or sauces.

Steaming Rack

This round rack, preferably made of metal, resembles a cake rack. It is used to elevate plates of food above the boiling water in a wok while steaming. Bamboo or metal steamers with two tiers and a cover are also available, but unless a lot of food is steamed, a wok and steaming rack is sufficient.

Deep-Frying Thermometer

This handy device will ensure the exact oil temperature used in recipes calling for deep-frying.

Cooking Chopsticks

These are longer than ordinary eating chopsticks. They are made of bamboo and come in various lengths. Choose the proper length by the comfort and ease of handling best suited to you.

How to use

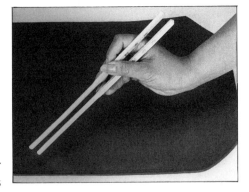

1. Rest the first chopstick on top of your ring finger with the thumb braced over the chopstick.
2. Hold the other chopstick as you would a pencil.
3. With the inside chopstick held stationary with your thumb, move the outside chopstick, forming pinchers to pick up ingredients.

Cleaver

The basic Chinese knife is the cleaver. It is used for cutting recipe ingredients and in the same motion, transporting them to an awaiting wok or serving tray. The cleaver usually measures 3-4inch(8-10cm) wide and 8inch(20cm) long. The thickness varies from thin cleavers for vegetable slicing all the way to thick bone-chopping cleavers. A sharp cleaver is necessary to perform the various cutting methods discussed in the cooking methods section. Keep your cleaver sharp by using a sharpening stone and steel as often as needed.

MENU PLANNING

In serving a Chinese meal, there is no single main course as in the typical American meal, but a combination of courses to be presented simultaneously for everyone to enjoy. The Chinese serve two different types of meals depending upon the occasion and circumstances. The formal banquet dinner is appropriate for a larger group of people celebrating a special event while the more common informal dinner is more of a practical everyday meal. The recipes and emphasis of this book are directed toward the successful preparation of an informal Chinese meal and I would strongly suggest mastering the preparation of an informal dinner before attempting to serve a banquet.

A formal Chinese banquet is served to a gathering of ten or more guests customarily seated around a large round table with a revolving "Lazy Susan" in the center of the table for easy access to individual dinner courses by the guests. The banquet would normally consist of ten courses served in a particular order by a staff of servants. A large platter of cold meat and vegetable appetizers is usually first to arrive. Then follows two to four stir-fried dishes. The bauquet always includes a hot soup which may be served at any point in the banquet, but traditionally near the end of the meal. The premier entrees such as a whole duck or fish would follow the stir-fried dishes. Rice or noodles would then be served to complete the banquet. All the dishes are brought out in quick succession to insure that all courses are hot and delicious. Finally, tea is served to end the banquet. Wine may also be served throughout the entire meal. The Chinese banquet is very elaborate and as such, should be reserved for very special occasions.

The informal Chinese dinner is more appropriatly suited for the life styles of today. Nutritious, economical, and easy to prepare, Chinese food is most of all delicious. Therefore, I have devoted this book to the preparation of dishes used in an everyday Chinese meal. The informal dinner is designed for a party of four people. In any event, keep the group to less than ten people unless you plan to serve a buffet style dinner.

Planning your menu is the important first step in preparing the meal. Always prepare as much in advance as possible so as to be able to enjoy your company instead of being stuck in the kitchen. It is also a good practice to try a recipe before cooking it for guests. Always read the entire recipe before starting to cook.

MENU CHART

Number of People Served :	2	4	6	8	10
Course					
APPETIZER	*	*	*	*	*
SOUP	*	*	*	*	*
RICE or NOODLE	*	*	*	*	*
(Allow ½ cup uncooked or 1½ cups cooked rice per person)					
MEAT-BEEF	1	1	1	1	1
-CHICKEN			1	1	1
-PORK				1	1
(Selection of beef, chicken, or pork dish is up to you)					
SEAFOOD		1	1	1	1
VEGETABLE	1	1	1½	2	2½ or 3
DESSERT	*	*	*	*	*
(Usually fresh fruit)					

*ADJUST RECIPE FOR NUMBER OF PEOPLE

Continued on page 106

Continued from page 105

The menu chart of page 105 illustrates sample menus for varying groups of people. For instance, an informal meal for four people would consist of one each of an appetizer, soup, rice or noodle, meat of your choice, seafood, and vegetable dish.

Generally, rice always accompanies a Chinese meal. Dessert is usually fresh fruit in season and tea is served at the end of the meal.

For every two additional people, i.e., 6, 8, 10, add one meat dish of your choice and increase the vegetable selection by ½ recipe. Rather than increase the recipe, you may prefer to make two different vegetable dishes. When in doubt as to how much food to prepare, remember it is far better to have leftovers than to run short of food at the dinner table.

When planning your menu, always consider the balance of flavors, the required ingredients, and cutting/ cooking methods previously mentioned. Incorporate different meats and vegetables to vary the menu. For example, cook one dish of chicken, one dish of beef, and one dish of pork instead of three chicken dishes.

However, you may also economize by working the menu around one major roast or meat. By using a pork loin end roast for instance, portions of the roast can be cut for barbecued pork or sweet and sour pork. Bits and pieces of pork may further be used in the making of won ton filling or chow mein. The remaining bones may then be simmered for an excellent soup stock. Even the last bits of cooked pork on the bones can be removed and used in fried rice or egg fu yung. This efficient and economical use of meat also applies to the use of a whole chicken. Whenever possible, balance the menu by serving a different meat dish or use different meats in the vegetable dishes. You can always save what is not used for another meal with the aid of a freezer to preserve your meats.

The greatest in Chinese cooking are your resourcefulness, ingenuity, and ability to adapt in the face of unavailable ingredients. Shopping for weekly specials at your grocery store and preparing your menu accordingly will save you money. Of course, you may always choose to increase a recipe rather than prepare two separate recipes which will necessitate a shorter list of required ingredients.

GLOSSARY

Anise, star

Brown, eight pointed star shaped seed with the taste of licorice. Used as a flavoring for sauces. Keeps indefinitely on shelf.

Bamboo shoot

Cream colored, cone shaped shoots of bamboo. Canned shoots are most common. Once opened, store covered with fresh water up to 1 week in the refrigerator. Change water frequently. Does not freeze well.

Bean curd, dried sheets or rolls

Sold in sheets or rolls. Soak in hot water until soft, rinse and cut into desired size before using. Flat sheets can be deep fried, and soaked in hot water to soften before use. The sheets become tougher, but will not dissolve with longer cooking, such as in braised dishes. Do not soak sheets in water before deep frying.

Bean curd, fermented (fu yu)

Fermented white bean curd with a cheesy flavor. It is sold bottled in half inch thick squares. Keeps in refrigerator indefinitely after opening.

Bean curd, fresh (*tofu*)

Usually square shaped, creamy texture, bland curd made from soybeans. Also comes deep-fried and canned. Fresh bean curd, covered with water, can be kept in the refrigerator for approximately one week. Remove from original package and replace with fresh water as soon as possible. Change water every 2 days to keep fresh.

Bean curd, red (nam yu)

Sometimes called wet bean curd. Red soft cubes of fermented bean curd with a strong cheesy flavor. Comes in cans. Once opened, store in jars with a tight lid in the refrigerator indefinitely.

Bean filling, sweet

Thick sweet bean paste made from beans and sugar. Often used as a filling for pastries. Usually sold in cans. Store tightly covered in refrigerator or in freezer indefinitely.

Bean sauce, brown or yellow

Sauce made from soybeans and salt. Often comes in cans. Some bean sauces may contain bean halves and others may be a smooth sauce, similar to Japanese red *miso*, which can be used as a substitute in some recipes. Keeps indefinitely in the refrigerator in a tightly sealed jar.

Bean threads (saifun or cellophane noodles)

Thin, long, dry noodles made of mung bean flour. Keeps on shelf indefinitely. Soak in warm water for 15 minutes before use. May also be deep-fried in hot oil. Do not soak in water if used for deep-frying. Use as a noodle in soups or with stir fried vegetables and meats. To keep clean up to a minimum, place noodles in a large paper bag before removing wrapper. Break off amount needed and store remainder in bag.

Bean paste, hot (soy bean paste with crushed red chili)

Soybean sauce made from soybeans, chili peppers and sometimes garlic. Comes in cans or jars. Refrigerated, keeps indefinitely in tightly sealed jars. Degree of hotness may vary between different brands. Brown soybean sauce combined with a hot sauce or crushed red chill can be used as a substitute.

Bean sprouts

Sprouts of the mung bean: about 2inch(5cm) long. Refrigerate sprouts covered with water. Keeps for one week. Change the water often.

Bitter melon

Long, green, pear shaped melon with a rideged surface. It has a definite bitter taste. Cut melon in half lengthwise and remove seeds. Cut in thin slices and stir-fry with meats.

Continued on page 108

Continued from page 107

Black beans, fermented

Salted, fermented, soft black bean seed. Mainly used to flavor sauces. Rinse with water before using. Keeps in a covered container on the shelf indefinitely.

Black bean sauce with chili

Salted, fermented black beans combined with hot chili peppers often found in paste form.

Bok choy (Chinese cabbage or greens)

Dark green leafy vegetable with a white stalk. Keeps in refrigerator for one week. High in vitamins A and C.

Broccoli, Chinese

A tender, green, seasonal vegetable available in spring and summer months. Chinese broccoli is more slender and leafy than regular broccoli. For recipes in this book, substitute with bok choy, spinach, or regular broccoli cut into long slender pieces.

Cleaver

The knife used to do most cutting in Chinese cooking. Usually a lighter, thinner cleaver is used for slicing and chopping meats and vegetables. The heavier cleaver is used to cut through bone.

Cloud ears

Brown, irregular, leafy shaped fungus or mushroom with a delicate taste. Soak 15 minutes in warm water to soften. Rinse, remove hard knobs on bottom of ear before using. Keeps indefinitely on shelf when dried. Also called tree ears.

Five spice

Blend of five ground spices: Szechuan peppercorns, anise, cinnamon, fennel and cloves. keeps on shelf for several months.

Ginger root

Irregular bulb, (rhizome) of the ginger plant. Hot and spicy in taste. Slice ginger and freeze separated slices. Keeps in the freezer indefinitely. Peel ginger and store in rice wine, or simply wrap air tight container and store in refrigerator.
Slice and use as needed.

Hairy melon (jit gwa)

Oval shaped, green melon with a hairy surface. Peel, slice thin and use in soup.

Hoisin sauce

Pungent, sweet condiment sauce made of soybeans, spices, chili and sugar. Once opened, store in a jar with tight lid. Keeps refrigerated for about 6 months.

Jelly fish

Body of the jelly fish cut into shreds. Usually sold salted and packaged in plastic bags in the refrigerator section. Store in refrigerator or freezer. Rinse off salt and soak in cold water before using.

Litchi nuts

A sweet, white fruit about 1 inch(2.5cm) in diameter. It has a dark red hull which must be removed before eating. Also comes canned and dried. use as garnish or as a fruit.

Long beans, Chinese

Foot long, thin green beans. When cooked, resemble string beans but have a more delicate flavor. Treat in same manner as regular green beans, but requires much less cooking time.

Maifun (rice noodles)

Noodles made from rice flour. Soak until soft in hot water before using. Also, noodles may be deep-fried in hot oil. Do not soak before deep-frying. To keep clean up to a minimum, place package of noodles in a large paper bag before removing wrapper. Break off amounts as needed. Store remainder in the bag.

Mirin

Japanese sweet rice wine used in cooking to bring out flavor or to add a little sweetness. Not interchangeable with rice wine.

Miso

Fermented bean paste made from soybeans and rice. Used mainly in Japanese cooking. Red or *aka miso* is saltier and white or *shiro miso* is milder or sweeter.　Red *miso* is a good substitute for brown bean sauce. Refrigerate *miso* in sealed containers indefinitely.

Mushroom, dried (forest or black)

Dried black forest mushrooms have a delicate flavor.　Can be stored in covered container on the shelf, indefinitely.　Must soak in warm water until soft.　rinse,　discard stem and use in recipe.

Mustard, dried

Pungent powder.　When mixed with water,　forms sauce which is used as a dip to accompany barbecued pork and other foods.　Store dry powder on shelf indefinitely.　Mix 1 T water to 1 T dry powder for average proportion.

Orange peel

Dried peel of tangerines.　Used for flavoring meats and other dishes.　To prepare:　Thoroughly clean skin of tangerine,　peel into sections,　cut away pulp and allow skin to sun dry.　Make sure skin is free of pesticides if making your own dried skins.

Oyster sauce

Thick brown sauce made from oysters and soy sauce.　Used to enhance flavor or as a dip.　Keeps indefinitely in the refrigerator.

Panko (dehydrated bread crumbs)

Japanese dehydrated bread crumbs with a coarser texture than regular bread crumbs.　Available at most supermarkets or oriental groceries.　To make *panko*,　use white bread and make coarse crumbs in the blender.　The dry crumbs slightly in the oven.　Then,　dry crumbs slightly in oven.

Parsley, Chinese (Coriander or cilantro)

A leafy parsley with a pungent flavor.　Use as a garnish.　Also may be used to add flavor to most any dish.

Plum sauce

A sauce made from plums and apricots combined with vinegar,　sugar and chili pepper.　Use as a dip for roast duck or meat dishes.

Rice

Long grain is most popular among southern Chinese.　Calrose,　medium grain rice can be used as substitute.　Glutinous rice is very sticky when cooked and is use for sweets.　Refer to rice section for more information.

Sausage, Chinese (Lop cheong)

Cured pork sausages about　6inches(15cm)　in length with a sweet flavor.　Refrigerate up to one month or freeze up to several months.

Seaweed, dried

Dried seaweed is usually available in sheets.　Keeps indefinitely on the shelf.　Some seaweed sheets are more expensive because they are roasted and seasoned.　These are used in Japanese cuisine for *sushi*.

Sesame seed oil

Golden brown oil of toasted sesame seeds.　Buy in small quantities and keep refrigerated after opening. Add to dishes just before serving,　loses flavor when heated.

Shrimp, dried

Dried tiny shrimp.　Soak in warm water for about　½　hour to soften before use.　Keeps on shelf indefinitely in covered jars.

Snow ear

White fungus or mushroom.　Comes dried and must be soaked in warm water before use.　Remove hard knobs from bottom of ears.　Keeps dried indefinitely.

Snow peas (Chinese pea pods)

Flat edible pea pod.　Has a delicate taste and comes fresh or frozen.　Must string as in green beans before cooking.

Soy sauce

The extract of fermented soybeans combined with salt.　Soy sauce range from light to dark.　Light soy sauce is the most delicate,　and is used as dip or in cooking;　gives little color.　Some dark soy sauce has caramel added for color and is slightly sweet.　Japanese soy sauce is in the middle and serves most

Continued on page　110

Continued from page 109

purposes very well. For most recipes, Japanese soy sauce may be used unless specified differently in a recipe.

Stir-fry

This technique can be applied to any combination of meats and vegetables. Seafood is also delicious. Refer to stir fry in information section section of book.

Szechuan peppercorns (fagara)

Dried berry of the prickly ash. It is not hot but has a slow numbing effect. Lightly toast in fry pan; finely crush to a powder. Strain through a fine mesh strainer to filter coarse outer shell.

Szechuan vegetable

The knobby bulb of a radish preserved in chili pepper and salt. Rinse before using. Store airtight in jar. Refrigerate or freeze indefinitely. No substitutes.

Tiger lily flowers

Dried golden brown tiger lily flowers; about 2inches(5cm) long. Soak in warm water about 15 minutes and rinse, remove hard stem before use. Keeps indefinetly on shelf when dry.

Thickening, cornstarch and water

Cornstarch and water is the most popular mixture used to thicken a sauce. Dissolve 1 tablespoon of cornstarch in 1 tablespoons of water. Use as needed to thicken sauce to the desired consistency. Always bring sauce to a full boil and then thoroughly combine ingredients together.

Freshest ingredients of the season, attention to the technique of stir frying, cooking just until crisp and tender and most importantly consistent and organized.

Tonkatsu sauce

Japanese prepared sauce used as a dip for tonkatsu, a pork cutlet.

Turnip, Chinese (lo bok or daikon)

Crisp large white root vegetable resembling a large carrot. peel skin and slice or shred before using. Store in refrigerator.

Turnip, salted-turnip

Sliced and preserved with salt. Rinse off salt before using. Often used in fillings or sliced and steamed with pork. Keeps in tightly sealed jar indefinitely.

Vinegar, rice

A mild vinegar made from rice. Used in most oriental dishes. Keeps indefinetly on shelf.

Water chestnuts

Walnut size, brown bulb. Must be peeled before use. It is sweet and has a crisp texture similar to apples. Canned water chestnuts are peeled and boiled. They will keep, if covered with fresh water in the refrigerator for about 2 weeks. Change the water frequently.

Wine lees

A thick fermented wine paste. Light miso (Japanese soybean paste) can be used as a substitute.

Wine, Shaohsing or rice

Chinese rice wine used for drinking. or cooking. Dry sherry may be used as a substitute.

Winter melon (tung gwa)

A large light green melon with a white powdery surface resembling a water melon. The inside is white with seeds in the center. Usually sold in sections. Peel hard skin and discard seeds. Slice melon and use in soups.

Wok

A wok is a metal pan with sloping sides and a rounded or flat bottom. The 14inch(35cm) wok is the best size for home use. Refer to wok in the information section of this book (page 103).

Won tons

Fresh squares of noodle. Usually comes in one pound packages. Thickness varies from thick to thin. Fresh won tons will keep in the refrigerator for one week. Can be frozen, wrapped airtight, for about 2 months. Use thick wrappers for deep fried won tons. Thin wrappers are better for soups.

I N D E X